C000183903

INTRODUCTION

The Guide The aim of this guide to the pilgrim route through central and southern France is to provide brief details of the itinerary, places of particular interest and where to eat and sleep between Le Puy-en-Velay and Saint-Jean-Pied-de-Port. It is thus not intended to *replace* but to *accompany* existing route-finding guides.

This guide does not cater specifically for any one group, whether walkers, cyclists, riders, motorists or people using public transport. However, places which welcome those on foot or travelling by bicycle are included wherever possible.

The walkers' route is waymarked throughout with the red and white *balises* of the French GR (*Grande Randonnée*) network, though the GR65 and the historic pilgrim route do not always coincide. It is **NOT** suitable even for mountain bikes and in many sections these are prohibited, the cyclists' route following minor roads for the most part. In general this is a strenuous route, especially in the Aubrac, so take this into account when planning your pilgrimage.

Getting to and from Le Puy and principal places along the route
a) By train: the quickest way is to go by TGV to Saint-Etienne. If you take the 07.23 Eurostar you will reach Le Puy the same day at 17.25. Le Puy can also be reached by TGV from Paris (Gare de Lyon), changing at Saint-Etienne (where there are two railway stations: the Le Puy trains leave from SNCF Carnot, several trains a day).
  If you are doing the Le Puy route in sections you can travel to/from *Cahors* by train to/from Paris (Gare d'Austerlitz, on the Toulouse line). *Figeac* can be reached by train from Paris via Aurillac or Toulouse, *Moissac* from Agen, Bordeaux and Toulouse and Paris via Montauban. *Saint- Jean- Pied-de-Port* is easily reached (or left) by local train to Bayonne (3-4 services a day), from where you can return by train to Paris (TGV).

If you are taking a bicycle, however, life is much more difficult and arrangements for cyclists are becoming progressively more complicated. You cannot travel on main-line SNCF trains or a TGV with your bike and it is no longer possible to register it through in advance to Le Puy from London Victoria or Dover because the ferry companies will not accept unaccompanied bicycles. Sealink ferries will carry your bike free of charge, providing you are with it, but if you do not want to ride it from either Calais or Dieppe to Le Puy you will then have to register it with SNCF at Calais-Ville, who will send it independently of you since French trains do not have guards vans (and a delay of up to 5 days can be expected until it is ready for collection at Le Puy). However, recent pilgrims have reported taking bikes free on other (e.g. regional) French trains as *bagages à main* (hand luggage)or *bagages accompagnés*. It is suggested that you read both the booklet *The Rail Traveller's Guide to Biking by Train* (for UK travel) and the latest edition of *Bicycles on French Railways,* obtainable from French Railways at 179 Piccadilly, London W1V OBA, if you are thinking of taking a bike to Le Puy by train.

b) **By air:** Ryan Air operates a service both to *Saint-Etienne* and *Biarritz* (5km from Bayonne railway station) i.e. you can fly to one place and return from the other, and you can also take bicycles. This is not only much quicker but is likely to be much cheaper too (a 2001 cycling pilgrim reports paying as little as £19 *return* from Britain, for both himself and his bike!!!).

c) **By coach**: Eurolines operate a regular coach service from London (Victoria Coach Station) to *Lyon,* from where you can travel to Le Puy by train. There are 4 services a week to Lyon all year with extra ones in summer, leaving at 18.00 and arriving in Lyon (by the Lyon Perrache railway station) the following morning at 8.45am. You can then take the train to Le Puy, changing in Saint-Etienne (often a delay), 2h.15mins travel time. However, do not buy a return ticket, even if you are only doing a relatively short section in France, as getting back to Lyon from points along the route is very complicated; rather than stop in Conques, for example, you will find it much simpler to continue for two days more to Figeac and take the train from there to Brive and then either the train to Paris or a Eurolines coach (on the Toulouse line) direct to London. Eurolines also operates a (less frequent) service to *Saint-Etienne* (on the Clermont-Ferrand line).

If you are doing the Le Puy route in sections you can travel to (or from) *Cahors* by coach (Eurolines runs a twice-weekly service to Toulouse, Wed/ Sat through the year, plus Mondays in summer, leaving at 20.00 and arriving in Cahors the following day at 14.15). From *Saint- Jean- Pied-de-Port* take the local train to Bayonne (3-4 services a day), from where you can connect with the Eurolines coach direct to London (book this well ahead if travelling in July or August).

Alternatively, if you are planning to walk the French part of the route one year and the Spanish the next, you will probably find it easier, rather than stopping (and restarting) in Saint-Jean-Pied-de-Port, to continue (for two to two and a half days more) to Pamplona and break your journey there. Public transport is readily available from (and to) Pamplona from places such as Madrid, Barcelona, Irún and Bilbao as well as the Eurolines direct bus service to London, and you will be fit after 4-5 weeks walking and have no difficulty crossing the Pyrenees. If you then complete the Spanish part of the route at a later date, when you are probably not yet so fit, you will find it physically easier (i.e. flatter) and more enjoyable than beginning with the long uphill slog from Saint-Jean-Pied-de-Port on your first day.

Cyclists have two other options.   a) The European Bike Express, a comfortable coach with a trailer to carry the cycles, either to Lyon or to/from Bayonne as well as a new drop-off point 10km north of Saint-Etienne. They have 15 pick-up points between Middlesbrough and Dover. Contact them at: 31 Baker Street, Middlesbrough, TS1 2LF, or on (01642) 251440 (reservations), fax: (01264) 232209.   b) The Dutch cycle bus service from Woerden (near Rotterdam) to Dax (or Burgos).   Details from Fietsvakantiewinkel, Jan de Bakkerstraat 14, 3441 EE Woerden, Holland.   (Tel: 0031 (0)3480 21844; they speak English.)

Luggage transport services
Some *chambre d'hôte* and hotel proprietors now transport walkers' luggage to their next overnight stopping place but, with the increasing popularity of the Le Puy route, two firms now operate a regular service covering the entire route from Le Puy to Saint-Jean-Pied-de-Port so that those who prefer to walk without a rucksack (or not a heavy one with all their possesions in it) can do so for a fee per item per stage.   Both also offer the possibility of returning you by car/minibus to your starting point early in the day when they have finished delivering luggage. Pilgrims wishing to avail themselves of this service should contact the firms direct (in French? info. welcome):

a) *Transbagages,* 18 Allée des Soupirs, 48000 Mende.   Tel (and fax): 04.66.65.27.75 (answer machine) or transbagages@wanadoo.fr.   This firm operates between Le Puy and Cahors and all main intermediate places and will also return people from Conques to Le Puy, Conques to Aumont-Aubrac and Cahors to Aumont-Aubrac.
b) *Factage* Tel: 05.63.94.75.60 (after 3pm) mainly coves the scond par of the route, as far as Saint-Jean-Pied-de-Port and includes places in between such as Cahors, Moissac, Lectoure and Eauze, with the possibility of returning pilgrims to their starting point.   They also have an emergency mobile phone number: 06.72.17.76.54.

Maps   Michelin 919 is a single map covering the whole of southern France. Cyclists can choose between the Michelin 1:200,000 series   (75,76,78,79 and 85)   and the IGN (Institut Géographique National) green series. The latter are recommended for walkers as the GR65 and its variants are marked on them. The scale is 1:100.000 (i.e. 1cm = 1km) and only 5 are required (as against 25 in the blue 1:25.000 series): 50(5),58, 57(4), 63(3) and 69. This series is widely available in Britain but a leading map shop in London is Stanfords, 12 Long Acre, Covent Garden, WC2E 9LP (020 7836 1321), www.stanfords.co.uk. You can order by post (or visit, of course) from The Map Shop, 15 High Street, Upton-upon-Severn, Worcs., WR8 0HJ (01684 - 593146), www.themapshop.co.uk, or by e-mail from the Hereford Map Centre (01432 266 322): mapped@globalnet.co.uk.

Guides There are now several different ones available, both in English and in French.

There are two guides in English, both published by Cicerone Press. One is for walkers: Alison Raju, *The Way of St. James: Le Puy to the Pyrenees* (2003, £11.00). The other is for (touring) cyclists (on surfaced roads): John Higginson, *The Way of St. James: Le Puy to Santiago - A Cyclist's Guide* (1999, £8.99). Both guides contain detailed route descriptions as well as practical and historical information and are "pilgrim-oriented" in their approach.

Stanfords stock the *Topo-Guides des Sentiers de Grande Randonnée*, the French GR guides with text and b/w maps on facing pages but **make sure you get the latest edition.** The set for the Le Puy route along the GR65, entitled *Le Sentier de Saint-Jacques*, was originally in 4 parts but is now in 3; the first volume covers the section from Le Puy to Figeac, the second from Figeac to Moissac, including the GR651 and GR36 variants along the valley of the Célé and the third the route from Moissac to Roncevaux. These guides require a good command of French but also contain interesting local historical and other information though some pilgrims have found that their route descriptions are not detailed enough. They are also not particularly "pilgrim-oriented" either, catering more for walkers on holiday doing only a section of the entire route than for pilgrims who are using the GR65 in order to walk all the way from Le Puy to Saint-Jean-Pied-de-Port and beyond; as a result the *balises* often lead you on "scenic detours" (not infrequently involving very steep climbs) either to avoid even short stretches of (minor) road or to descend to a town (the entry to Saint-Côme d'Olt is a case in point) with a plunging view of it (which you will not see anyway in bad weather or appreciate if you are already exhausted). If you are using these *topoguides* make sure you read through your daily section well ahead of time so that you can work out more direct alternatives if you need to, from the (good) maps they provide.

Louis Laborde-Balen & Rob Day, *Le Chemin de St-Jacques du Puy-en-Velay à Roncevaux par le GR65*, Randonnées Pyrénéennes/FFRP, has more extensive route descriptions and coloured maps (the *Route Historique* as well as the GR65) with more information on places of interest and has been updated several times but is printed on very heavy paper (and weighs nearly half a kilo!). It is readily available in France (e.g. from the extensive bookshop section of Au

Vieux Campeur, a very large walking equipment store: 2, rue Latran, Paris 5e (01.53.10.48.27), branches of the FNAC or from bookshops in Le Puy but you may need to order it in Britain. They also stock the so-called "Dodo guide," a French, annually-updated publication with practical facilities along the Le Puy route. This is somewhat curiously entitled *Miam-Miam-Dodo: Le Chemin de Compostelle* (the first three words translating something like "yum-yum-bye-byes") and can be obtained from bookshops, several gîtes along the way or directly from the author: Jacques Clouteau, Editons du Vieux Crayon, 119 Route de l'Aubraie, 85100 Les Sables d'Olonne (02.51.90.84.97, fax: 02.51.90.85.55, email j.clouteau@wanadoo.fr).

Pilgrims who read French may also be interested in a small, pocket-size (A6) booklet entitled *En Chemin vers Saint-Jacques: guide spirituel du pèlerin*. As its title suggests, it is intended as spiritual aid and contains themes for personal meditation, prayers and hymns, notes on the many saints whose churches, chapels and sanctuaries line the route as well as other information likely to be of help to the pilgrim. Copies are available from the Confraternity and it is also on sale in Le Puy (in the cathedral sacristy), in Conques, Estaing and in some churches along the way. A guide to *Haltes Chrétiennes* along the Le Puy route is also in preparation (info. welcome - available in Le Puy?)

Accommodation is not a problem now on the Le Puy route and it is possible to walk the entire route staying in *gîtes d'étape* (see below) without having to cover enormous distances. Likewise those who prefer to stay in hotels and/or *chambres d'hôte* will have no trouble as the latter, especially, are becoming increasing available in villages. Most towns, even small, have a campsite, and many farms along the way offer *camping à la ferme*. (Pilgrims who prefer to stay in hotels are referred to a list prepared by a member of the Confraternity, a copy of which is available from their office, and they will also find the "Dodo guide" referred to above very helpful, as will pilgrims on horseback.) *Gîtes d'étape* contain simple, dormitory-type accommodation, at least one hot shower and cooking facilities and cost between 5 and 12 euros per person in 2003, with a small extra charge in many cases if the heating is on in cold weather. (*Relais d'étape* is the same except that you cannot cook; anything less falls into the category of *refuge* or *abri*.(shelter)) Blankets are normally provided so only a sheet sleeping bag is needed. The *gîtes d'étape* (as opposed to other types of *gîte*) are for walkers, cyclists and riders only but unlike youth hostels you do not need to be a member of an organisation to use them. There are now plenty within easy walking distance of each other (e.g. every 15km or so) as far as Conques though after that they are often further apart (e.g. 25km). Many are municipally-run (*gîte communal*) and will contain all the above facilities but in other places establishments that call themselves *gîtes d'étape* are in fact only *relais* as they provide no cooking facilities and few opportunities, for example, to wash clothes; these are often run by restaurants, hotels or bed and breakfast places that attach a dormitory and showers and provide meals if required but not the rest of the facilities you would expect in a "proper" *gîte d'étape* and may also be more expensive. This does not mean that their standards are low but that pilgrims on a budget should be on their guard. There are now many *gîtes d'étape* along the Le Puy route though the newer ones are often quite small and, with the growing popularity of this route (pilgrim numbers increasing at a rate of 20% per year), it is becoming increasing necessary to book ahead from June to September (as unlike the *refugios* in Spain the gîtes in France will rarely put people on the floor or find other ways of accommodating surplus pilgrims). At other times of the year it is also advisable to phone the day before in popular areas, especially at holiday times or on weekends with a *pont* (i.e. a public holiday on a Thursday or a Tuesday when people take Friday or Monday off as well) as walking clubs, for example, and other groups, sometimes book (and pay for) the whole *gîte*, even if they do not always fill it; in such cases it is usually possible to sleep there once you are actually on the spot, though good French will be needed to negotiate. *Gîtes d'étape* may seem too spartan for some people's tastes but they are a very good way to meet and get to know other pilgrims, as are the *refugios* in Spain, especially if you are walking or cycling the entire route.

> *Note:* there have been problems in recent years with people making reservations and then not notifying the *gîte* owners when they do not intend to use their bookings. Please remember to ring ahead if you have to cancel.

Campsites vary in price according to the facilities they offer but, as more and more sites are being upgraded, there are fewer simple ones than there used to be and it may often be very little cheaper to camp than to stay in a *gîte d'étape*; the only real advantage in carrying a tent is the freedom to stop where and when you want to as campsites are so numerous. In addition, there is now some pilgrim-only accommodation along the Le Puy route, the beginnings of a network paralleling that to be found on the *Camino francés* in Spain and these places are indicated in the relevant sections of this guide. Some *gîtes d'étape* are only open from Easter to October and most campsites are closed in winter. A hotel offering a *forfait pèlerin* (or *soirée étape*) has a special rate for dinner, bed and breakfast.

Pilgrim Passport
Walkers, riders and cyclists who are members of the Confraternity can obtain, via its office, a pilgrim record or "passport". This is a document which you can now get stamped (*tamponné*) without any difficulty at churches, town halls (*mairies*), tourist offices etc., as well as most *gîtes d'étape* and campsites along the way as proof of your journey. It will also help you obtain your Compostela

from the Cathedral authorities there if you continue on through Spain to Santiago. The French *Créanciale* (pilgrim record), issued by the Eglise de France, is available (in person only) from the sacristy in the Cathedral in Le Puy while the one provided by the French pilgrim associations is available from the Amis du Puy (see below under "Le Puy" in *The route and where to stay* section).

Other practical points

Shops (for food) are open till 12.00 or 12.30 and then from 14.30 or 15.00 until about 19.00. Those in small villages are usually shut not only on Sundays but often on Monday mornings (and sometimes afternoons) as well, so considerable organisation is needed when following the GR65 since this not only avoids towns but does not always enter the villages it passes either - you may often have to leave the route to go shopping. Remember, too, that there are more bank holidays (*jours fériés*) in France than in Britain, when all shops apart from bakeries will be closed: e.g. May 1st, 8th, Ascension Day, July 14th, August 15th, Nov. 1st and 11th.

Meals are available between 12.00 - 13.30 and 19.00 - 20.30. If you are a vegetarian you will probably find life very difficult if you want to eat out.

Telephones More and more public telephones in France operate with *télécartes* (phone cards), except in rural areas. All phone numbers in France now consist of 10 digits, as 01, 02, 03 04 or 05 have been placed at the start of the previous eight figure numbers. (06 is used for mobile phones). Please note that if you phone from Britain you do not use the "0", in the same way that you omit it when calling Britain from abroad. The new emergency number in France (for all services) is now 112.

Changing money Most post offices in France now provide a money-changing service, even in quite small places, and these are open much longer hours than banks. There are also an increasing number of "hole-in-the-wall" cash dispensing machines (*distributeurs de billets de banque*), even in fairly small towns, and which accept VISA, Cirrus cards, etc. These are indicated (where known) by the abbreviation "CD" in this guide and information on the existence of others would be welcome for the next edition.

Planning the day It is important to plan each day, using this guide, your route-finding guide and your map. The walker's route from Le Puy to the Pyrenees is one of the most strenuous of the pilgrim roads through France and temperatures in July/August can exceed 100ºF. In such cases it is advisable to leave as soon as it is light in the morning and arrive at your destination, or at a place to rest up, by late lunchtime. Museums and other places of interest (frequently closed on Tuesdays) are normally open until 7pm so you can visit them in the early evening. Start with shortish distances to begin with (this is easy to do if starting from Le Puy as there is plenty of accommodation) and gradually increase them. Avoid too tight a schedule and build in enough rest days.

Snakes have been reported by several pilgrims on the stretch from Le Puy to Cahors and also between Saint-Palais and Saint-Jean-Pied-de-Port. They may not be very common but if you do meet them (usually when it has been very hot for a while) it will be when you are off your guard... (Stick useful.)

Note for walkers   Since many pilgrims are not experienced walkers the following suggestions are given to help ensure a more enjoyable journey, with trouble-free feet and back. They are also directed to the Confraternity's booklet *The Walking Pilgrim*. (A parallel publication is available for **cyclists**.)

a) **Before you leave** Start walking regularly at least 6 months beforehand - join a rambling club if possible as they have walks of different lengths/speeds to allow you to build up your stamina. This way you can walk in nice places with (usually) friendly people, have a leader who knows the way and good places to walk, rather than just along the streets of where you live. Then increase the distance, number and size of hills and the amount and weight of luggage you take until you can carry what you need. After that it is essential to go out walking on at least 2 days in a row, with *all* your gear; walking 15 or 20 miles on a "one-off" basis is a very different matter from getting up again the following morning, probably stiff and footsore, and starting out all over again.

b) **Equipment** *Boots/shoes* - buy these well in advance and break them in before you leave. If carrying your own luggage, don't take *anything* (except waterproofs, first aid and pullover) that you won't use every single day: leave out anything that "might come in useful." *Sheet sleeping bag* (for *gîtes*). *Comfortable rucksack*, not more than 50 litres unless carrying a tent; if you borrow one, make sure its owner is the same height/build as yourself, choose one with a wide waist/hip belt and internal frame and avoid the "ladder" type - they are very uncomfortable. Make sure, too, that you use a large plastic bag or strong bin-liner inside as no rucksacks are waterproof, however expensive/high quality they may be. *Stick* is a great asset for fending off dogs (a constant nuisance on the GR65) and testing boggy terrain. *Guide book, maps* and *dictionary* (small) if needed. *Compass* (if you know how to use it), *torch, large water bottle* (2 litres for July/August). *First aid kit* with elastoplas/microporet by metre, scissors, needle (for draining blisters: "second-skin" products or Dr. Scholl's adhesive foam useful to prevent them). *Waterproofs*: "poncho" type with space for rucksack inside best for summer when anorak/cagoule is far too hot; if possible get one with front zip (try Decathlon). *Sunhat*. If you are prone to sunburn a high factor *sunscreen* (e.g. factor 20) is advisable in summer (Tshirt with collar useful for protecting back of neck). A *knife, fork, spoon* and *plastic mug* are also very useful.

Note for cyclists Hills are steep and long so you will need a low gear in the high twenties or low thirties. If you have British size wheels take a spare tyre (and spokes) and even if you have a Continental one take two spare inner tubes. Take a small amount of oil with you as the heat soon dries out the bearings. Do not take any unnecessary clothing or equipment: you may have to push it up a lot of hills. Pilgrims who are not used to cycling or who are out of practice are also advised to train before they leave, in order to enjoy their journey. A note from a former pilgrim reminds fellow cyclists to eat well too, despite the possible heat, in order to be able to tackle the route's many steep sections. Information regarding the whereabouts of cycle repair shops is given where known

Language It may seem so obvious as not to need pointing out but don't expect *anybody* (repeat: anybody at all!) to speak English. Assume you will have to speak French at all times, for everything you need, however complicated. If you are not already fluent, consider including a year's evening classes in your preparations; if you are unable to communicate easily you will feel very isolated in the 4-5 weeks it takes to walk from Le Puy to the Pyrenees and what will make or mar the journey, after problems of physical fitness, will be the extent to which you can (or can't) talk to other walkers and pilgrims, to local people and to deal with possibly complex situations.

Poste restante If you want to send things to yourself further along the route (e.g. maps and guides) or have people write to you you can do this via the *poste restante* system whereby you collect your mail at the Post Office. Address the letter/parcel to yourself (surname first), Poste Restante, postal code and name of town. The most likely places you will need will be the following: 43000 Le Puy-en-Velay, 46100 Figeac, 46000 Cahors, 82200 Moissac, 40800 Aire sur l'Adour and 64220 Saint-Jean-Pied-de-Port. There is a small fee for each item collected and they only keep them for 15 days before returning them to the sender. (In Spain, however, the same service - the *Lista de Correos* - is free and items are kept for one month before being sent back.)

Abbreviations Gîte = *gîte d'étape*, CD = cash dispenser, PTT = Post Office, CH = *chambre d'hôte*, L = left, R = right, KSO = Keep Straight On, CRS = cycle repair shop.

Prices refer to 2003. *To convert francs to euros a convenient rule-of-thumb is to add half the amount and then divide by ten; e.g. 70FF + 35 = 105 ÷ 10 = 10 Euros. Gîtes d'étape*, as already indicated, charge between 5 and 12 euros per person. Hotels and *chambres d'hôte*, in general, range from 35 to 60 euros (and beyond), according to the category, for two people sharing a room.

Finally, for pilgrims who attend mass and who would like to be able to join in at least once during the service the **Lord's Prayer** is given below in French:

Notre Père qui es aux cieux,
que ton nom soit sanctifié,
que ton règne vienne,
que ta volonté soit faite
sur la terre comme au ciel.
Donne-nous aujourd'hui
notre pain de ce jour.
Pardonne-nous nos offenses,
comme nous pardonnons aussi
à ceux qui nous ont offensés.
Et ne nous soumets pas à la tentation,
mais délivre-nous du Mal.

* * * * * * *

Bonne route et bon pèlerinage

THE ROUTE AND WHERE TO STAY

Figures (in brackets)after a place name indicate its distance in km from both Le Puy and Saint-Jean-Pied-de-Port, preceded by its height in metres and population where known.

Le Puy-en-Velay 625m (0/740) Population 29,000. All facilities. SNCF (trains from Paris via Lyon and Saint-Etienne or Clermont-Ferrand and Saint-Georges d'Aurac). Gîte d'étape (near cathedral) for pilgrims and walkers in the Maison Saint-François (04.71.05.96.86, 19pl.), Rue Mayol, open all year. Another gîte d'étape is on the route out of town at 29 Rue de Capucins (04.71.04.28.74, 19pl.). Youth Hostel (04.71.05.52.40, closed w/ends 31/10 - 31/3) in Centre Pierre Cardinal, Rue Jules Vallès, also in upper part of town, as is the Accueil Saint-Georges, Grand Séminaire, 4 Rue Saint-Georges, which also takes pilgrims (open all year). Campsite (Camping municipal de Bouthezard), Chemin de Roderie is to NW of town, on an island in river (Easter to October 15th). Several hotels from 1 to 3 star including Hôtel le Régional, 36 Bd Fayolle, cheap (04.71.09.37.74), as is Etap Hôtel, 25 Av. Charles Dupuy (opp. station, 04.71.02.46.22) and Hôtel Bristol, 7 Av. Maréchal Foch (04.71.09.13.38).

> *Note:* book ahead if you intend to start mid-September, the time of the "Fête du Roi de l'Oiseau."

Pilgrim stamp available from the cathedral sacristy (10-12, 14-18). Mass in cathedral at 07.00 every morning (conducted by the Bishop of Le Puy whenever possible), followed by pilgrim blessing (stamp also available then). The "Amis du Puy," many of them former pilgrims, hold an information session with a *verre d'amitié* (drink) every evening from Easter to November, 18-19.30, at 29 Rue Cardinal de Polignac (in old part of town), where they also issue (and stamp) pilgrim passports.

An ancient town in a volcanic landscape, Le Puy is dominated by rocky peaks rising from the valley floor. One is crowned by the chapel of Saint-Michel d'Aiguilhe (the Needle), built by Godescalc, Bishop of Le Puy after his pilgrimage to Santiago in AD 951 (worth climbing the 267 steps to visit it). Romanesque Cathedral of Notre-Dame, now fully restored, is surrounded by the narrow twisting streets of the old town, with many interesting houses. Inside the cathedral: 11th-12th c. cloisters and statue of the Black Virgin. (Black Virgins were once thought to have originated only from Africa but it is now thought that they are also local and "black" because of a life of hard work in the fields and the open air.) Statue of St. James the pilgrim on pillar inside cathedral (to RH side facing altar). Enormous statue of Notre-Dame de France overlooks the town from a rock high above it. Worth spending at least half a day to visit Le Puy. Ask at tourist office (Place du Breuil) for a walking tour plan of the town. Musée Crozatier. Eglise du Collège, first "Jesuit-style" church in France, 13th c. Eglise

Saint-Laurent, Chapelle des Pénitents, Baptistère Saint-Jean, Chapel of Monastère Sainte-Claire, Tour Pannessac. Statue of St. James the pilgrim in niche above chemist's shop on corner of Rue Saint-Jacques.

Le Puy has been a pilgrimage centre since the Middle Ages, not merely as a starting (or assembly) point for French pilgrims and the many "feeder" routes and/or those coming from further afield but also in its own right. Pilgrimages to Notre-Dame du Puy began in the 10th century and the shrine has its own "Jubilee" years, those in which the Feast of the Annunciation (March 25th) coincides with Good Friday. The first was in 992 (thus predating the first Holy Year in Santiago, in 1179) and is the third oldest after Jerusalem and Rome. There have been three such Jubilee years in the 20th century - 1910, 1921 and 1932 - and the next, the thirtieth, falls on March 25th 2005. Le Puy is also famous for its bobbin-lace making and its (brown) lentils.

8km Saint-Christophe-sur-Dolaison 908m (8/732)
2 cafés (the one by church has restaurant), phone box, PTT. CH at Tallode, 0.5km, Mme Allègre (04.71.03.17.78), gîte de groupe.
12th c. church built of pink rock.

6.5km Chapelle Saint Roch (14.5/725.5) *Early 13th c. Romanesque chapel, the first of many along the way dedicated to the patron saint of pilgrims. It was originally dedicated to St. James, then Saint-Bonnet (a local saint) and then, in the 17th century, to Saint-Roch. Inside there are two engravings of Saint-Roch as a pilgrim and one statue. Chapel is normally open.*

0.5km Montbonnet 1108m (15/725) Gîte d'étape with camping place
adjacent (04.71.57.50.82 and 06.82.83.89.18, 20pl., open all year). Gîte d"etape l'Escole Philippe Grde, 04.71.57.51.03).Bar (does food).

[**Bains**, on alternative route, is 1.5km NW of Augeac. Shops, cafés, restaurant. CH (Mme Raveyre, 04.71.57.51.79 & 06.83.59.93.47) and Hôtel-restaurant Archer (04.71.57.52.38, open all year). Church of Sainte-Foy de Conques.]

7km Saint-Privat d'Allier 890m (22/718) Shops, hotel, gîte d'étape
(04.71.57.25.50, open 1/3 - 1/11), municipal campsite (04.71.57.22.13, May - October), bars, boulangerie, tourist office, fountain. Hôtel de la Vieille Auberge, (04.71.57.20.56). *Gothic church (Saint-Privat was a local saint), remains of château.*

3km Rochegude 967m (25/715) Tower, tiny chapel dedicated to St.
James perched on top of rocky belvedere.
Note: Both the descent down to and the ascent out of Monistrol are very steep and may be slippery in wet weather.

3km Monistrol d'Allier 619m (28/712) SNCF (Paris-Clermont-Ferrand-Arvant-Nîmes), Hotel-Restaurant des Gorges (04.71.57.24.50), CH. Municipal gîte d'étape at Centre d'Accueil (1.5km before village on Le Puy road, 04.71.57.22.22, eve., 33pl., open all year). Halte Randonneur Gîte "La Tsabone" (04.71.57.24.85, 10pl., open all year). Municipal campsite by river (1/4 - 15/9). *Romanesque church, former priory of La Chaise-Dieu: cross has carving of headless pilgrim.*

12km Saugues 960m (40/700) Pop. 2,000. Hotels, bars, restaurants, shops, 2 banks (+CD), post office, tourist office, 2 gîtes d'étape, one municipal (at campsite, 04.71.77.80.62, 12 pl., 1/4 - 15/10), one next to CH Rue des Roches (Mme Itier-Martins, 04.71.77.83.45., reported good); accommodation (+ meals if required) at Centre d'Accueil, Rue des Tours Neuves (04.71.77.60.97, 120pl. CH (M Gauthier, 04..71.77.86.92). Hôtel de la Terrasse 04.71.77.83.10) and Hôtel des Tours Neuves (04.71.77.82.60) Campsite (15/6 - 15/9).

Romanesque church of St. Médard (and treasury), diorama de St. Bénilde (a local saint), 13th c. Tour des Anglais with dungeon, numerous old houses. Saugues was the meeting point of pilgrims coming from the Auvergne via secondary routes and had a 12th c. pilgrim hospital (now an old people's home near the Chapelle des Pénitents) dedicated to St. James and with large statue of St. James inside.

9.5km Le Falzet 1134m (49.5/690.5) Gîte d'étape (04.71.74.42.28,6pl, open all year *except* July and August).

[**Chanaleilles**, 10 mins off GR from **Contaldès**, has church worth visiting, shop; ask in café (does meals, 04.71.74.41.63) to sleep in gîte d'étape, 15 euros.]

9.5km Domaine du Sauvage 1292m (59/681) Gîte d'étape (04.71.74.40.30, 20 pl.) at farm in listed building (produce for sale, meals possible if you phone ahead, otherwise provide your own food, cooking facilities, open all year).

3km Chapelle-Saint Roch 1280m (62/678) *Also known as Chapelle de l'Hospitalet du Sauvage. This was a hospital for pilgrims and travellers founded at this col in 1198, originally dedicated to St. James (chapel was next to present fountain). The chapel was rededicated to Saint-Roch after the Wars of Religion (1562-98) but then fell into ruin. The new chapel built at the end of the 19th century was destroyed by a cyclone in 1897 and the present one was rebuilt in 1901. Usually locked but a grille in the door enables you to see inside. Statue of Saint-Roch with his dog above the altar. Sunday mass 11.15 am July to September. Refuge on road (clean and well-kept, fountain at rear) a useful place to rest, eat or shelter in bad weather.*

La Roche-de-Lajo (just off route on D14 and GR4): CH (Mme Jalbert, 04.66.31.52.07, 14pl., all year, reported good). Also Mme Astruc (tel: 04.66.31.53.22, 4-5pl., open all year, she no longer provides meals but you can cook your own).

Les Faux (10 min. off route to L, section where GR65 and GR4 coincide briefly) gîte d'étape M. Parent (04.66.31.50.09, 19pl., open all year).

10.5km Saint-Alban-sur-Limagnole 950m (72.5/667.5) Small town (pop. 2,000) with shops, restaurants, bars, gîte d'étape on top floor of Hôtel-restaurant du Centre (04.66.31.50.04, 18 pl., open all year), bank (with CD), tourist office in château courtyard. Hôtel-restaurant du Breuil (04.66.3.51.76). Campsite at end of town (1/3 - 15/11), 500m after GR turn-off.

Romanesque church of Saint-Alban in town centre (red sandstone and polychrome brick). Château (various dates) is now part of the regional psychiatric hospital.

7.5km Les Estrets 940m (80/660) Gîte d'étape (04.66.31.27.74, 12 pl., 1/4 - 15/10, also CH), phone box, fountain.

Formerly a commandery of the order of St. John of Jerusalem, controlling the passage over the Truyère; hence its name - "étroits," i.e. "straights." Present church dates from 1866, replacing previous one (though plaque on wall refers to "chapelles" being rebuilt); statue of Saint-Roch inside and lectern has carvings of scallop shell, scrip and pilgrim staff.

9km Aumont-Aubrac 1050m (89/651) Small town (pop. 1,050) with 4 hotels including Relais de Peyre (04.66.42.85.88), Hôtel-restaurant Astruc (04.66.42.81.71) & Hôtel Prunière (04.66.42.80.14); Bar/Hôtel Calypso also has rooms. Shops, cafés, bank (CD by post office). Gîte d'étape at entrance to the town, 9 Rue du Barri (41 pl., open all year). Spartan accommodation with cooking facilities in parish hall (by church, phone first: 04.66.42.90.25, no charge as such but leave a donation). New private gîte reported attached to Aubrac Hôtel (04.66.42.99.00). Municipal campsite (July-August), SNCF (Paris - Montpellier line: train service now replaced by buses).

Former Benedictine Priory and Romanesque church of Saint-Etienne; restored in 1994 it now has splendid modern stained glass windows.

4.5km La Chaze-du-Peyre 1040m (93.5/646.5) Phone box, fountain, new public toilets. *Two crosses in square in front of church, one 18th century, the other 19th. Church of varying periods with St. James' chapel.*

Note: After this the Aubrac plateau starts; warm clothing advised (including gloves) except July/August.

6.5km Les Quatre Chemins 1174m (100/640) Café "Chez Régine" (picnic with own food possible if purchasing a drink), also CH and caravans per night.

[**Prinsuéjols**, (1205m, 3km due south on GR du Pays known as the "Tour des Monts d'Aubrac," waymarked with red and yellow *balises*) has gîte détape (04.66.32.52.94, 40pl.) and bar/restaurant. You do not need to retrace your steps the following morning but can take the D73 northwards from Prinsuéjols in the direction of *Malbouzon*, passing through the hamlet of *Pratviala*: this road crosses the GR65 further to the west, just after the Ferme des Gentianes.]

4.5km Ferme des Gentianes 1192m (104.5/635.5) Farm does meals and CH (Mme Corriger, 04.66.32.52.82, reported good).

8km Montgros 1234m (112.5/627.5) Private gîte "Maison de Rosalie" (04.66.32.55.14, no cooking facilities), also auberge (meals, rooms, café; expensive but food reported good).

3.5km Nasbinals 1180m (116/624) Shops, cafés, restaurants, bank (but no CD), municipal gîte (04.66.32.59.47, 19 pl., 1/4-31/10), private gîte (La Grappière, 04.66.32.15.60, 15 pl., 15 euros w/bkfst, cooking possible, 15/3 - 31/10) and gîte in Centre d'Accueil (04.66.32.50.42, 48pl., open all year); equestrian gîte (open all year), municipal campsite 25/5 - 30/9). Hôtel La Randonée (04.66.32.54.07), Hôtel Le Bastide (04.66.32.56.82), Hôtel La Route d'Argent (04.66.32.50.03), Hôtel de France (04.66.32.50.19). Tourist office, pharmacy, bank, boulangerie, épicerie, bars.
11th c. Romanesque church in local stone and style (Statues of St. James (modern) and Saint-Roch inside). The monument with a pair of crutches on its base is to Pierre Brioude ("Pierrounet", a 19th c. bonesetter and manipulator of joints who is said to have treated over 10,000 people a year.)

9km Aubrac 1307m (125/615) Restaurants, bars (no shops). Gîte d'étape (16pl., July-August only) in Tour des Anglais (access via tourist office, 05.65.44.21.15). Large barn/shelter reported on one side of square in village, the "Grange des Pèlerins Perdus" ; unattended but provides shelter, cooking facilities and means to make hot drinks - run by village to help pilgrims when gîte is closed during the day. "Village de Vacances Royal-Aubrac", a former sanatorium to R on road 500m before the village of Aubrac, 05.65.44.28.41, open all year, also accepts pilgrim if places available. Hôtel-Restaurant de la Domerie (05.65.44.28.42).
12th c. Domerie d'Aubrac, village founded in 1120 by a Flemish knight, Adelard de Flandres, who was attacked there by bandits on his way to Santiago and who almost died there in a storm on his return journey. In gratitude for his deliverance he founded Aubrac as a place of refuge for pilgrims. Church of

Notre-Dame des Pauvres is all that remains of the monastery, plus one other building. Tour des Anglais, botanical garden.

From here you have the option of a 25km waymarked route direct to **Espalion** via the Cistercian **Abbaye de Bonneval** (simple gîte d'étape, 6pl., in its Tour Saint Jacques).

8km Saint-Chély-d'Aubrac 808m (133/607) Small town with restaurants, shop, tourist office, PTT but no bank. Municipal gîte détape (05.65.44.28.34, 19pl.), gîte d'étape (M. Martin, 05.65.44.26.25, 35pl, open all year), municipal campsite (15/6 - 31/8). Hôtel des Voyageurs (05.65.44.27.05) and Hôtel de la Vallée (05.65.44.27.40). Bar/rest. on main street run by M. Lefèvre also has rooms.

15th c. church has statue of St. Roch. 16th c. cross on old bridge over the Boralde with tiny pilgrim sculpted in its base, with his stick and rosary.

20km Saint Côme d'Olt 385m (153/587) Hotel, shops, restaurant, PTT, gîte d'étape with stables in building behind Tour de Greffe (former prison, 0672.52.29.97, 19pl., open all year, key at hardware shop opp. boulangerie). Campsite (1/5 - 30/9, also rents caravans per night). Hôtel des Voyageurs (05.65.44.05.83). Tourist office.

Olt is the old name for the river Lot. Medieval town with very few modern buildings. 16th c. church of SS Côme and Damien has twisted spire, 10th c. Chapelle des Pénitents, formerly with pilgrim hospital dedicated to Saint James adjoining, Ouradou (pilgrim oratory). 15th and 16th c. houses, 14th c. château is now Hôtel de Ville, Gothic bridge. Historic information on street plaques: walking tour available from tourist office.

After 1km along the river outside Saint- Côme and after bridge you now have a choice between a strenuous high-level detour (LH fork but not waymarked immediately) to visit the *Vierge Notre-Dame de Vermus*, a viewpoint over the whole of the Lot valley with a statue of the Virgin on the top, worth the climb in splendid, dry, weather but not otherwise, or continuing along the road (waymarked) and thus go directly to Espalion but missing out the Eglise de Perse.

5km Eglise de Perse 353m (158/582) *Romanesque chapel of Saint-Hilarion (built on site near where he was beheaded by the Saracens in the 8th century) in red stone, former pilgrim halt and priory affiliated to Conques. Very fine carvings on outside. Not normally open but push-button entry on door at side reported. NB. the waymarked route does not actually take you to the church so turn L at new sports centre and it is 500m from there.*

1km Espalion 342m (159/581) Busy town (pop. 4,614) with 2 hotels, shops, cafés, restaurants. Gîte d'étape on 3rd floor of Maison du Foyer Marie Couderc (05.65.44.07.24, 19 pl., open all year); gîte d'étape communal, (5 Rue St. Joseph, 11 euros, 05.65.51.10.30 and 06.77.58.53.08). Gîte-type accommodation (no cooking) also available (except July & August) in VVF (colonie de vacances) 1.5km outside town on GR65 (05.65.44.02.15, 1/3 - 30/11). Hôtel Moderne (05.65.44.05.11, bikes stored in garage), Hôtel de France (05.65.44.06.13). Campsite Bellerive, Rue du Téral (1/5 - 30/9, also has caravans to rent per night).

Pilgrim bridge over the Lot, built in the reign of Saint-Louis by the Frères Pontiff (a monastic bridge-building order). Renaissance château (1572) and Musée Vaylet, local museum (no longer contains statue or painting of St. James).

3km Eglise de Saint-Pierre-de-Bessuéjouls 335m (162/578) *One of the oldest churches on the route, 11th c. chapel of Saint-Michel on first floor of bell tower, with 9th c. altar.* Good picnic place outside.

6km Verrières (168/572) Bar (summer only?).

2km Estaing 320m (170/570) Small town (pop. 1,000) with all facilities. Hospitalité Saint-Jacques, Rue du Collège (05.65.44.19.00) is a small lay community established to look after pilgrims on their way to Santiago, 16 place gîte, open all year; meals taken with the community (bkft after 7.45 service), lauds, rosary and compline each day. No charge as such but pilgrims should consider leaving a donation. Gîte d'étape in former chapel (05.65.44.71.74, 20pl., open all year, key from Mme Breçon in Café du Château on NW corner of bridge). Municipal campsite 2)m north of town on D167. Two hotels: Aux Armes d'Estaing (05.65.44.70.020 and Auberge Saint-Fleuret (05.65.44.01.44).

Gothic bridge over the Lot. 15th c. château of the Counts of Estaing is now a convent (mass daily). 15th c. church of Sainte Fleuret has stone cross outside depicting tiny pilgrim and gilded statue of St. James inside.

Note: energetic pilgrims have the option of a (4km) shorter route to Conques on the old GR6 via **Saint-Genies des Ers, Campuac** (modern church with fine stained glass) and **Larrigue**, rejoining the GR65 in *Campagnac*, 3.5km before Espeyrac. To take this option leave Estaing on minor road (marked "Campuac") to LH side of chapel at end of bridge.

16km Golinhac 650m (186/554) Shop, bar/restaurant, gîte d'étape (05.65.44.50.73, 19pl., open all year), campsite (May-September) are all on L at entry to village. Gîte équestre, fountain, in hamlet of **Le Radal** 500m before Golinhac and gîte/CH 2km away at **Le Battadou** (good reports).

Church of Saint-Martin (statue of Saint-Roch with coquilles (scallops) inside) on site of foundations of 9th c. Benedictine abbey (note cross at entry to village with tiny pilgrim and staff on base).

8.5km Espeyrac 369m (194.5/545.5) Café, epicerie (behind hotel). Municipal gîte d'étape (12 pl.) behind Mairie (05.65.72.93.46 or 05.65.69.87.46,1/4-1/11). Hôtel-restaurant de la Vallée (05.65.69.87.61). Fountain/tap by church.

Church of Saint-Pierre has statue of Saint-Roch inside and, like the church of Saint- Chély d'Aubrac, has an unusual statue of St. Peter with cockerel at his feet.

3.5km Sénergues 506m (198/542) Hotel, 3 bars, restaurant (not open all year), bakery, superette, PTT and other shops. Private gîte d'étape in Domaine de Sénos, large house on LH side of road at entry to village (05.65.72.91.56, 36pl., not open all year, also CH).

Church of Saint-Martin (statue of Saint-Roch inside on back wall, nice modern stained glass windows) on site of 9th c. priory (shady square at side is a good place for a rest). Tour Carré.

6km Saint-Marcel 570m (204/536) *Church of Saint-Marcel (a pope, martyred in 309) but nothing is left of the original Romanesque building except the chapel; the present church was rebuilt in 1561 but only finally finished in 1875. The statue of Saint-Roch as a pilgrim, with hat, scallop shells, stick and gourd that was inside the church when the previous edition of this guide was prepared seems to have disappeared. Stained glass window above door has three scallop shells. There was a leprosarium here in the 17th and 18th centuries and a Chapelle Saint-Roch built in 1629, i.e. at the height of the plague. This is the original pilgrim route, which ran along the ridge before descending to Conques in the valley below.*

3.5km Conques 280m (207.5/532.5) Shops, restaurants. PTT but no bank. Accueil Abbaye Sainte-Foy (behind abbey church) has dormitory accommodation (3-tier bunks) for pilgrims plus rooms (05.65.69.85.12, 80pl., open all year), municipal gîte d'étape in former *gendarmerie* near church (05.65.72.82.98, 24 pl.); key from Mme Guibert, Résidence Dadon (wooden relief of Saint James on door), rue Emile Rondié. Camping Beau Rivage by river (April - September). Hôtel-restaurant Saint-Jacques (05.65.72.86.36) and Auberge du Pont Romain (meals, rooms, 06.65.69.84.07, by river).

Note: accommodation is often a problem in Conques, now that the Le Puy route has become so popular; book ahead if possible or arrive early in the day.

Mass with pilgrim blessing in abbey church in evenings (check times).

If you are finishing in Conques there is a subsidised taxi service (*Transports à la demande*) to the railway station at Saint-Christophe (from where you can travel, without changing, to Paris), cost 10 euros: ask at tourist office or phone

Mme Lample (05.65.72.90.03). For a service to Rodez station (direct travel to Paris), 8 euros, phone M. Bouscal (05.65.69.86.01).

Important pilgrim halt with Romanesque abbey church of Sainte-Foy and adjoining treasury, Pont romain (medieval bridge) over the Dourdou. Conques survives almost intact since the Middle Ages and the whole town is a historic monument. Very "touristy" but a good place for a rest day after first stage of journey. Go up to 16th c. chapel of Saint-Roch for good view over town. The whole town is a historic monument so the balises *are very discreet: wooden squares, carved, so watch out carefully for them.*

1.5km Chapelle Sainte-Foy (209/531) *Site of a local pilgrimage, chapel built by a spring whose waters were reputed for miraculous cures for eye complaints. Modern stained glass window of Saint James as pilgrim inside.*

4km Noailhac (213/527) Gîte d'étape (05.65.72.91.25, 18pl., open all year) also CH, key to gîte in Café-Restaurant Chemin Saint-Jacques.

3km Chapelle Saint-Roch 595m (216/524) Picnic area; splendid views looking over Conques in valley below.

Chapel has statue of Saint-Roch as a pilgrim outside in the tympanum above the door and another inside above the altar as a non-pilgrim. The chapel is the focus of a local annual pilgrimage every year on August 16th, Saint-Roch's day; this began between 1847-49 when, due to a typhoid epidemic, a procession of local people made its way to the top of the hill (path now lined with Stations of the Cross), where public prayers were addressed to the saint, invoking his help. As a result the number of those inflicted with the disease is reported to have decreased rapidly and the custom has continued ever since. The chapel was built on the site in 1884.

11km Decazeville 225m (227/513) Medium-sized town (pop. 7,000) with all facilities. Hôtel Moderne (05.65.43.04.33) and Hôtel Foulquier (05.65.63.27.42) but no gîte d'étape, SNCF. (If you intend to sleep in Livinhac on a Monday buy food here.)

The town takes its present name from the Duc de Decazes, minister of industry under Napoleon and responsible for the promotion of large-scale mining in this area. Decazeville has the largest opencast coalmine in Europe, La Découverte (visits possible).

2km Eglise Saint-Roch 353m (229/511) *A parish church, rather than the usual chapel or hermitage dedicated to this saint. Three statues of him inside the church, one above the main altar in full pilgrim gear, another large statue as pilgrim but minus hat, in side chapel, and a third small (alabaster?) statue of the saint as a non-pilgrim at the side of the altar in the side chapel. There is also a modern drawing of Saint-Roch the pilgrim* en chemin, *walking with* *his dog by his side in front of the chapel at Noailhac, but here his cloak is down and his wound covered up as he is on the move.*

2km Livinhac-le-Haut 220m (231/509) Café, bakery, shop, PTT, gîte d'étape above Club des Toujours Jeunes, key + PS from Bar de la Mairie (05.65.63.33.84 & 05.65.63.33.85, 22pl., open all year), campsite by river (with restaurant, rents caravans per night, 1/4 - 30/9), CH/mini-gîte "Chez Robertson" (05.65.33.93.94, open all year).

6km Montredon 396m (237/503) Bar/épicerie, gîte d'étape (05.65.50.10.57, 2pl, Easter to 1/11), CH (Mme Debray, 05.65.34.38.20).
   Hilltop village with Chapelle Notre-Dame at cross roads (replaces older chapel) and church of Saint-Michel on site of former priory.

3km Chapelle de Guirande 277m (240/500) *Romanesque chapel of Sainte-Madeleine with late 14th c. murals (for key try electricity box).* Gîte équestre and *camping à la ferme* 300m away at **Le Communal** (05.65.50.10.45, 25pl., Easter to 1/11, reports vary as to standard).

6km Saint-Félix (246/494)
Restaurant: does midday meals if pre-booked (05.65.50.14.01)
   Romanesque church of Sainte-Radegonde has Adam and Eve with tree and serpent on its 11th c.tympanum. Later stained glass window of Saint James.

4.5km Carrefour des Sentiers 327m (250.5/489.5) This is the junction with the GR6A, where you have the option of a) turning R to go into **Figeac** or b) continuing ahead here straight to **La Cassagnole** (gîte d'étape) via the GR6A (large Leclerc superstore 500m further on on this route, with cafeteria and cash dispenser as well as food).

9.5km Figeac 194m (260/480) All facilities. SNCF (Paris, Aurillac, Toulouse), Small gîte d'étape at 26 Chemin de Bataillé, 10 mins walk from centre city, Mme Faivre-Pierret, open all year but ring ahead between Nov. 1st and Easter, 10.50 euros (05.65.50.01.83 or 06.81.96.22.21). Camping Le Rives du Célé (April - September) but no gîte d'étape. 8 hotels, including:
   Hôtel Le Toulouse (05.65.34.22.95),
   Hostellerie de l'Europe (05.65.34.10.16),
   Hôtel des Bains (05.65.34.10.89),
   Hôtel Pont du Pin (05.65.34.12.60), and
   Hôtel du Faubourg (05.56.34.21.82).
Busy town on river Célé (population 10,500) with network of restored medieval streets (ask in tourist office for walking tour leaflet), worth half a day's visit. Former abbey church of Saint-Sauveur, consecrated 1093, with ambulatory characteristic of pilgrim churches. Churches of N-D du Puy and Saint Thomas.

SUMMARY OF ST. JAMES AND PILGRIM REFERENCES
ON THE LE PUY ROUTE

Le Puy-en-Velay
- Statue of St. James by pillar to RH side of cathedral (facing altar).
- Tiny modern statue of pilgrim in niche above Hôtellerie du Fauçon, Rue des Farges.
- Statue of St. James in niche above chemist's shop on corner of Rue Saint-Jacques and Place du Plô.
- Musée Crozatier contains 2 paintings with St. James pilgrim in background, a woodcut of St. James pilgrim, a statue of Saint-Roch, a small collection of *coquilles* and statues originally housed in the former pilgrim hospital.
- Ceramic roundel (modern) of St. James and headless pilgrim on stone calvary along Rue Saint-Jacques leaving Le Puy.

Montbonnet   Chapelle Saint-Roch, early 13th c. Romanesque chapel, the first of many along the way dedicated to the patron saint of pilgrims. It was originally dedicated to St. James, then Saint-Bonnet (a local saint) and then, in the 17th century to Saint-Roch. (Many chapels originally dedicated to St. James changed their dedication due to Saint-Roch's success in curing plaque victims.) Chapel contains
- 2 engravings
- Statue of Saint-Roch pilgrim.

Rochegude
- Tiny chapel dedicated to St. James, perched on top of rocky belvedere.
- Wooden statue of St. James inside.

Monistrol d'Allier   Headless bas-relief of pilgrim on cross in churchyard of Saint-Marcellin.

Saugues
- Town was meeting point of pilgrims coming from the Auvergne via secondary routes and had 12th c. pilgrim hospital (now an old people's home near the Chapelle des Pénitents) dedicated to St. James.
- Large wooden polychrome statue of St. James inside (visits possible).
- Stained glass Saint-Roch in church of Saint-Médard and niche statue high up above west portal.
- Niche statue of Saint-Roch in nearby street
- "Tree" sculpture of pilgrims leaving Saugues by river.

Fontaine Saint-Roch   Site of a 13th c. oratory.

Chapelle Saint-Roch (3km after Domaine du Sauvage) Also known as Chapelle de l'Hospitalet du Sauvage; this was a hospital for pilgrims and travellers founded at this col in 1198, originally dedicated to St. James (chapel was next to present fountain). The chapel was rededicated to Saint-Roch after the Wars of Religion (1562-98) but then fell into ruin. The new chapel built at the end of the 19th was destroyed by a cyclone in 1897 and the present one rebuilt in 1901.
  * Statue of Saint-Roch with his dog above the altar (visible through the *grille* in the door).

Les Estrets Church contains
  * Statue of Saint- Roch inside.
  * Lectern has carvings of scallop shell, scrip and pilgrim staff.
  * Village formerly had a pilgrim hospital.

Aumont-Aubrac Niche of south wall of church of Saint-Etienne has shaft of cross with tiny pilgrim carved on it.

La Chaze-du-Peyre Church with
  * (Former?) St. James's chapel.
  * Statue of pilgrim-looking figure with coqille, blessing another figure.

Nasbinals 11th c. Romanesque church with
  * Statue of Saint-Roch
  * (Modern wood) Saint-Jacques inside.

Saint-Chély d'Aubrac
  * 15th c. church has stained glass and statue of Saint-Roch and statue of Saint-Jacques (among other apostles).
  * Old bridge over the river Boralde has 16th c. cross, with pilgrim sculpted in its base, with his stick and rosary.

Saint-Côme d'Olt
  * Pilgrim hospital dedicated to St. James adjoining Chapelle des Pénitents
  * Ouradou (pilgrim oratory).

Espalion
  * Pilgrim bridge over the Lot.
  * Stained glass St. Alaxius dressed as a pilgrim with staff and *coquilles* in parish church.

Estaing 15th c. church of Saint-Fleuret with
  * Stone cross outside depicting tiny pilgrim

- Gilded statue of St. James inside..

Golinhac
- Church of Saint-Martin has statue of Saint-Roch (with *coquilles*) inside [France has 3,674 churches dedicated to St. Martin!]
- Cross at entry to village has tiny pilgrim and staff on its base.

Espeyrac Church of Saint-Pierre has statue of Saint-Roch inside.

Sénergues Church of Saint-Martin has statue of Saint-Roch inside.

Fontromieu A farm whose name indicates the site of a former "pilgrim fountain."

Saint-Marcel
- Stained glass windows above door of church of Saint-Marcel has three scallop shells.
- Leprosarium here in 17th and 18th centuries
- Chapelle Saint-Roch built in 1629, i.e. at the height of the plague.
- In 1997 a statue of Saint-Roch was to be found inside the church (with hat, scallops, stick and gourd - i.e. as a pilgrim) but in 2001 it was no longer there - info. welcome.

Conques
- Chapelle Saint-Roch, perched on top of hill in lower town
- Modern wood Saint-Jacques in abbey church.
- Museum has painting of Saint-Roch in front of abbey church and statue of Saint-Roch.

Chapelle Sainte-Foy part way uphill leaving Conques has modern stained glass window inside depicting St. James the pilgrim.

Chapelle Saint-Roch (near Noailhac)
- Statue of Saint-Roch as pilgrim outside on tympanum.
- Another statue of the saint (not as a pilgrim) is inside, above the altar.

Chapelle Saint-Roch (2km after Decazeville) A parish church, rather than the usual chapel or hermitage dedicated to Saint-Roch.
- Two statues of the saint inside, one above the main altar in full pilgrim gear.
- Two other statues of the saint in the side chapel, one as a pilgrim (minus hat), the other a small alabaster figure as non-pilgrim, to side of altar.
- Modern drawing of Saint-Roch the pilgrim on the move, walking with his dog but his cloak down, covering his sore.

Saint-Félix Romanesque church of Sainte-Radegonde has later stained glass window of St. James.

Cajarc
- Pilgrim bridge over the Lot built in 1320
- Pilgrim hospital existed in 1269.

Cahors
- 15th c. cloister in cathedral of Saint-Etienne has sculpture of small pilgrim apparently disagreeing violently with another, non-identified figure.
- Cahors formerly had 4 hospitals (one dedicated to St. James) and a Chapelle de Saint-Jacques des Pénitents.

Moissac
- Ruins of Hôpital Saint-Jacques.
- Former church of St. James is now used as Musée Saint-Jacques.
- Bas-relief of Saint-Jacques (apostle) on corner pillar of abbey cloister.

Auvillar Rue Saint-Jacques.

Lectoure
- Cathedral of SS Gervais and Protais has stained glass window of St. James.
- Town formerly had a Hôpital Saint-Jacques

Marsolan Remains of Hôpital Saint-Jacques at entrance to village.

Chapelle d'Abrin Former pilgrim hospital (now a private house) at meeting of two routes (the other came from Rocamadour and Moissac via Agen).

La Romieu
- Village taking its name from the *romieux* (i.e. pilgrims) who passed through on their way to Santiago.
- Gilded bust of Saint-Jacques in Collégiale.

Condom
- Eglise Saint-Jacques on leaving town (statue over blocked up doorway is St. Joseph, not St. James), originally with a hospital behind it.
- Formerly there was also a second Hôpital Saint-Jacques nearby.

Pont d'Artigues Pilgrim hospital by the bridge over the river Osse, run by the Order of the Knights of Santiago in the Middle Ages.

Eauze
- Statue of Saint-Roch pilgrim in a side chapel in church of Saint-Luperc
- Stained glass Saint-Jacques in apse and stained glass Saint-Roch on south wall.

Manciet
- La Bonne Auberge (restaurant) is on the site of the former commandery (with Hôpital Saint-Jacques and chapel) set up by the Order of the Knights of Santiago.
- Modern statue of Saint-Jacques above church portal and statue of Saint-Roch inside.

Nogaro
- Romanesque church with former Hôpital Saint-Jacques nearby.
- Medieval paintings of pilgrims inside church of Saint-Nicolas.

Lanne-Soubiran Wooden polychrome statue of St. James the pilgrim in church of Saint-Pierre.

Eglise de Sensacq 11th c. church formerly dedicated to St. James.

Arzacq-Arraziguet Stained glass window of St. James in parish church of Saint-Pierre.

Louvigny Modern church of Saint-Martin has stained glass window with *coquille* and pilgrim staff and gourd.

Pomps Eglise Saint-Jacques (with statue of the saint).

Castillon Hospital for pilgrims and travellers in eleventh century.

Chapelle de Caubin Garden of restored Romanesque chapel contains sculpture recalling the passage of pilgrims en route to Santiago.

La Sauvelade Church of St. James (originally dedicated to St. Mary) is all that is left of monastery, with statue of St. James inside.

Navarrenx Church of Saint-Germain has pilgrim boss at base of ceiling vaulting near side chapel to RH side, with head with leather hat and scallop shell; three other heads believed to be of modern pilgrims.

Aroue Romanesque church of Saint-Etienne has 12th c. bas-reliefs of Santiago Matamoros in lintel of sacristy doors.

Saint-Palais Musée de la Basse-Navarre et des Chemins de Saint-Jacques de Compostelle contains statue of St. James pilgrim and much other historic pilgrim material from the region, including a copy of the bas-relief of Santiago Matamoros from Aroue church (which is often closed).

Larribar-Sorhapuru Shrine to R of four arch bridge over the Bidouze with small statue of St. James behind glass in a *stèle*.

Hiriburia Monument erected by the Société des Amis de Saint-Jacques to mark the place where the routes from Paris, Vézelay and Le Puy are thought to have met.

Harambeltz Statue of St. James inside chapel.

Ostabat-Asme Important pilgrim gathering point in past for those coming from or along different routes and its inns and hospitals could accommodate up to 5000 pilgrims; today only the Maison Ospitalia remains, as the present *gîte d'étape*.

Saint-Jean-Pied-de-Port
- Porte Saint-Jacques, through which pilgrims entered the town.
- Formerly there was also a Chapelle Saint-Jacques.

I would like to thank Marigold Fox for her assistance in compiling this summary.

NOTES

NOTES

Formerly an important pilgrim halt with six hospitals (one still exists). Musée Champollion (Egyptology), Musée du Vieux Figeac, Gothic Hôtel de la Monnaie, Maison des Templiers.

5km La Cassagnole 311m (265/475) Gîte d'étape (Relais Saint-Jacques, 05.65.34.03.08, M & Mme Lefrançois, 35pl., open all year, also rooms and CH. Bkft avail. but other meals only with prior notice. Small stock of basic food for sale). *Birthplace of Louis the Pious, son of Charlemagne and second Holy Roman emperor.*

3.5km Faycelles 319m (268.5/471.5) Bastide (walled) village with bar/restaurant/shop, CH (Mme Besse-Daynac, 05.65.34.07.66, on main street; kitchen?). Gîte facilities reported in presbytery (info. welcome).

500m before Mas de la Croix there is a gîte d'étape at *La Planquette,* (05.65.40.01.36, 10pl. + 8 in marquee in summer, campsite, April - September).

3.5km Mas de la Croix 327m (272/468) Here pilgrims have a choice between the historic route to Cahors via Limogne along the old Roman road *(Cami Ferrat)* over the *causse* (limestone plateau) and the GR651, the (waymarked) variant route along the Vallée de la Célé: see page 35 below.
  Shop and 2 restaurants in *Béduer* (0.8km ahead on variant route).

Ferme Auberge Domaine de Villedieu at *Boussac* (4km after Béduer), 1.5km off route (05.65.40.06.63).

HISTORIC ROUTE

9km Gréalou 374m (281/459) Hôtel des Quatre Vents (reported expensive, meals by reservation only, 05.65.40.68.71, bar). *Romanesque church of Notre-Dame de l'Assomption. There are a lot of dolmens in this area.*

4km Le Verdier 316m (285/455) Variant route through the woods to Cajarc starts here, 2km shorter and useful in bad weather (via the GR65A, waymarked with a diagonal white "bar" through the red and white *balises).*

6km Cajarc 160m (291/449) All facilities, gîte d'étape (06.14.66.54.89 or ask at nearby tourist office for key, 20 pl., open all year), municipal campsite (on the main GR65 out of town, May - September), Hôtel de la Promenade (05.65.40.61.21) and Auberge du Pont (05.65.40.67.84).
  Town situated in a "circus" of chalk cliffs. Pilgrim bridge over the Lot built in 1320 and a hospital existed in 1269. Chapelle de la Madeleine (only the chancel remains, known as "Chapelette de Cajarc" today, chapel of former 13th c. leprosarium.

Note: after Gaillac the *causse* begins, with no food or water until Cahors, except in Limogne, so stock up on both before leaving Cajarc.

20km Limogne-en-Quercy 300m (311/429) Small town with shops, cafés, restaurants. Gîte d'étape next to PTT (05.65.24.34.12, 19 pl., open all year or key from snack bar Le Galopin). Municipal campsite on edge of town (on D911, April - October). 2 CH: Mme Gavens (05.65.24.37.32) and Mme Dubrun (05.65.31.50.50).).

Gîte équestre 6km after Limogne at **Pech Ollié**, 900m off GR to R (signposted): M. Serre, 11pl, no cooking but meals available (phone first (05.65.31.59.57).

6km Junction with GR65B (317/423) KSO ahead here on GR65B to go into village of **Varaire** (café, shop, gîte d'étape, 05.65.31.53.85, 12 pl., 1/3 - 30/11).

To sleep in the gîte run by the nuns in the Monastère des Filles de Jésus in *Vaylats* (2.5km, 05.65.31.63.51, open all year, reservation *essential*, no cooking but evening meal provided; very welcoming, services at 6pm and 8am) turn L when GR65 crosses the D42, 3kms after *Bach* (Convent is in centre of the village). From the GR65B, by turning L onto the D19 when you reach this crossing. To continue the following morning you do not need to backtrack but can turn west along the D19 and after the last house (*after* the village exit board) a FP is waymarked "GR," leading you back onto the *Cami Ferrat*.

20km Junction near Le Pech (337/403) Gîte d'étape 500m to R at **Le Pech** (Mme Latour, 05.65.24.72.84, 16pl., 1/3 - 31/10).

13km Cahors 122m (350/390)

VALLEY OF THE CELE

This is not the historic route but a pleasant 54km variant along the river Célé until this runs into the Lot in Bouziès and where it joins the GR36. From here you can continue (west) for 21km along the common course of the GR36 and GR46 to rejoin the main GR65 in Les Bories-Basses. The routes are waymarked throughout with the usual red and white *balises*.

Béduer Fortress-like château English-owned and has art exhibitions. Shop, 2 restaurants, campsite (1/3-31-12) and gîte d'étape (April - September) 1km *before* village at **La Planquette** (05.65.40.01.36, 10pl plus 8 in *tente-marabout* (marquee) in summer). Just *after* **Béduer** there is a campsite (Camping Pech Hibert) which has chalets.

13km Espagnac Restaurant but no shops, municipal gîte d'étape (05.65.11.42.66, 20pl., open all year, 7, 9 or 11.50 euros). *13th c. Augustinian priory.*

4km Brengues Shop, 2 campsites (May-September), 2 CH: Mme Chanut (05.65.40.05.44) and M. Oulié (05.65.40.00.46). Hôtel-restaurant de la Vallée (05.65.4002.50).

4km Saint-Sulpice Shop, municipal campsite (April-September, with shop July-August). CH 1km off route (Mas de Jordy, 05.65.40.03.80, M. Raffy).

7km Marcilhac-sur-Célé Shop, restaurant, campsite, CH. 2 gîtes d'étape: a) municipal (05.65.40.61.43, 10pl., Easter-1/11) b) Mme Ménassol (also CH, 05.65.40.62.68, 15pl., open all year). Hôtel de la Promenade (05.65.40.65.58). 2 campsites.
Ruins of large Benedictine Abbey with statue of St. James in museum in Maison du Roy above tourist iffice. Numerous caves in area.
Another CH reported 3km along GR651: Mme Reusemann, Mas de Picarel (05.65.31.28.41).

9km Sauliac-sur-Célé *Château de Saint-Géniés.*

3.5km Château de Cuzals *Open-air museum of Quercy life (ethnology, agriculture, popular arts and traditions, etc.): allow plenty of time to visit.*

2.5km Espinières Info. welcome re. gîte, 22pl, plus tent-gîte in summer (14pl.), camping also possible (M. Rasseneur: 05.65.31.32.17).

4km Cabrerets Shop, restaurant, gîte d'étape (05.65.31.27.04, 17pl., also CH, Easter-November), campsite. 2 hotels (April-October only and both expensive): Hôtel des Grottes (05.65.311.27.02) and Auberge de la Sagne (05.65.31.26.62).
13th c. château of Duc de Biron (now privately owned), Château des Anglais in the cliffs. Prehistoric museum and Pech Merle cave system (well worth the stiff, 30 minute climb on the GR 651 to visit, allow about 2hrs).

7km Bouziès Hôtel-restaurant Les Falaises (05.65.31.26.83, expensive; April-October).
Here there is a further choice of route: *either* the alternative route to Cahors (walkers take the GR36 west) via **Galassie**,

(Hotel/restaurant still open?), **Vers**, Hôtel de la Truite Dorée (05.65.31.41.51.), campsite on D662, **Arcambal** with large 15th c. château, cafés. *or* south (walkers take GR36 *east*, as below).

4km Saint-Cirq-Lapopie Shop, municipal gîte d'étape (05.65.31.21.51, 23pl., 15/3-15/11), campsite, 2 hotels (both April to November only, both expensive): Hôtel de la Pélissaria (05.65.31.25.14) and L'Auberge du Sombral (05.65.31.26.08). CH reported 2km away at Tour de Faure (M & Mme Devot). *Fortified medieval hill village, perfectly preserved.*

10km Concots Shop.

7km Les Bories-Basses

15km Le Pech Gîte (see above, p. 22).

13km Cahors 122m (350/390) All facilities. SNCF (Paris-Toulouse-Port Bou), youth hostel in Foyer des Jeunes Travailleurs, 20 Rue Frédéric Suisse (near Mairie, 05.65.35.64.71, 40 pl., open all year, 8.85 euros, meals 7.80). Foyer des Jeunes du Quercy, 129 Rue Fondue-Haute (05.65.35.29.32, open all year, ring ahead) also puts up walkers/pilgrims. 10 hotels including:
Hôtel Le Melchior (05.65.35.03.38),
Hôtel de la Paix (05.65.35.03.40),
Hôtel Aux Perdreaux (05.65.35.03.50) and
Hôtel de la Bourse (05.65.35.17.78).
Camping Saint-Georges by river.
Large town (population 21,000) surrounded on three sides by the river Lot. Important pilgrim halt and a good place for a rest day. Cathedral of Saint-Etienne with cloisters (and carving of a first fight between pilgrims), several interesting churches and secular buildings. Pont Valentré (finest fortified bridge in Europe, note sculpture of devil on upper RH side of 2nd tower), museum. Ask in tourist office for a town plan with walking route.
Note: the GR65 does not enter the town centre.

Leaving Cahors: after crossing the Pont Valentré the waymarks of the GR65 lead you up a cliff face, *very* steeply uphill up narrow FP with steps (and handholds where the steps have worn away). However, although the steep section is not very long, if you have a large/heavy rucksack, if you are not very agile, if you don't like scrambling or if the weather is wet (and therefore slippery) you may prefer not to take the waymarked "passage sportif" up the cliffs. Instead you can turn *right* after crossing the bridge and follow the route waymarked in orange, using the road, and rejoin the GR65 1km at the top of the hill near the Croix de Magne, 223m, a very large cross, visible from the town below.

10km Labastide-Marnhac 257m (360/380) Phone box, fountain behind church. Camping à la ferme (April to August) near entrance to L.

L'Hospitalet 4km to SW of Labastide-Marnhac on variant GR65 has campsite open all year) and CH (Mme Daudé, 05.65.21.02.83).

13km Lascabanes 180m (373/367)
Pretty village with gîte d'étape (with very small shop) in former presbytery (adjoining church, 05.65.31.49.12 & 05.65.31.86.38, 17pl., open all year), CH (Mme Duler, Domaine de Saint-Géry, 05.65.31.82.51).
Lascabanes had a pilgrim hospital in the 15th century.

1km after Lascabanes on LH side of road you come to the chapel of *Saint-Jean-le-Froid,* with pilgrim book. Always open, good place for rest/shelter and has fountain 100m behind it. (Fête and Mass in Occitan last Sunday in June.)

CH at **Preniac,** signposted 1km off route (to R) and 4km before Montcuq, (Relais de Preniac, 05.65.31.88.51, reported good).

9km Montcuq (382/358) Shops, cafés, several restaurants. Gîte d'étape Le Souleillou, 500m before village, 30pl., kitchen, open all year, 9.50 - 11.50 euros acc. size of rooms (Jacques & Simone Lagane, 05.65.22.48.95). Municipal campsite (15/6-5/9) with tent available for pilgrims. Hôtel Saint-Jean (05.65.31.84.45), 2 CH: Mme Passemard (05.65.24.35.77) and Mme Toulet (05.65.24.90.78). Tourist office. Chimera bookshop on main street owned by two CSJ members.
Small hilltop town dominated by 12th c. keep. Church of Saint-Hilaire and a second church.

Note: 4km after Montcuq, after passing the Château de Charry you can fork L uphill off route from Berty 300m to visit church in **Rouillac** *(Romanesque frescoes on ceiling above altar): retrace your steps afterwards.*

14km Lauzerte (396/344) Shops, cafés, restaurants. Hôtel du Quercy (05.63.94.66.36, closed Sun. & Mon.), CH (Mme Basso-Chambon, Moulin de Tauran, 05.63.94.60.68). Tourist office, municipal gîte d'étape (05.63.94.61.94, 17 pl.), Camping Melving, open all year, also rents caravans per night (22pl.).
Bastide hill town dating from 12th century. Medieval houses, two churches (St. Barthélemy, with modern statue of St. James as pilgrim inside, and Eglise des Carmes).
3km Eglise Saint-Sernin du Bosc (399/341) *Church of Romanesque origin, restored 1991 onwards.*

5.5km Auberge de l'Aube-Nouvelle (404.5/335.5) Hotel-restaurant (05.63.04.50.33).

1.5km Durfort-Lacapalette 206m (406/334) Bar/tabac/grocery store, bakers, post office. CH and small dormitory, camping + tents to rent at *Besses*, 22/3-31/10; to walk thee continue on GR after Durfort then take 2nd minor road marked "Piquet" (Lynne & Howard Jones, 05.63.05.01.92).

Gîte (5pl.) & CH at **La Baysse**, S of Saint-Martin, ex. July/Aug., meals, (05.63.04.54.00).

Entering Moissac: be careful. After turning L onto the D957 there are 2 routes, both waymarked. a) For the standard route take the *5th* turning on the R (Chemin des Vignes). b) For the "scenic route" (i.e. the strenuous variant) take the *4th* turning R up the "C39 Chemin de Malengane." This takes you high up along a ridge before bringing you down via the Côte Saint-Michel into the old section of town by the public library (behind the abbey)

14.5km Moisssac 76m (420.5/319.5) All facilities. Pop.12,000 (twinned with Astorga, on the *Camino francés* in Spain). SNCF (trains to Agen, Bordeaux, Montauban, Toulouse). Large gîte d'étape in the Centre d'Accueil, 5 Sente du Calvaire, high up on hill above the abbey (05.63.04.62.21, 66pl., open all year). Pilgrims can also stay (phone first) at Presbytère, 20 bd. Camille Delthil (05.63.04.02.81 or 05.63.04.01.44, cooking facilities). Camping de l'Ile de Bidounet, 1km south of river (April-September). 4 hotels: Luxembourg (05.63.04.04.27), Le Chapon Fin (05.63.04.04.22), Récollets (05.63.04.25.44) and Le Pont Napoléon (05.63.04.01.55).

Major pilgrim halt from the Middle Ages onwards. Abbey church of Saint-Pierre, former Benedictine monastery founded in the 7th century with impressive cloisters; first built in 1100 they contain 116 columns and 76 capitals, 46 of which tell Bible stories or the lives of saints: a guided tour of the abbey is recommended. Musée Saint-Jacques is in the former church of St. James) Centre d'Art roman (Romanesque art) in former convent buildings to north of railway line near Abbey. Try to spend at least half a day to visit the town.

After Moissac there is a well-waymarked route along the canal towpath, before taking you over the bridge to cross the two canals and the river Garonne. This is the variant GR65 but neither it nor the high-level main one is the historic route, which passed south of the river (where the Autoroute des Deux Mers now runs).

11km Maulause (431.5/308.5) Bar/restaurant, shop in village itself). Picnic tables on RH bank by the 2nd (concrete) bridge. CH & gîte d'étape (Mme Granier, Le Grenier du Levant, 05.63.29.07.14, slightly off route but the owner will fetch you if you phone ahead).

3.5km Pommevic (435/305)   Bar, shop, 12th c. church in village, accessible by FP to R shortly before you reach the bridge.

4km Espalais (439/301) Shop.

1km Auvillar 108m (440/300)   Shops, cafés, restaurants. Municipal gîte d'étape in former presbytery with camping possible in its garden (05.63.39.57.33 & 05.63.39.89.82, 16pl., open all year, key from Mairie).   2nd gîte also reported.   2 CH: (Mme Sarraut, 05.63.39.62.45) & Mme Brehn (05.67.79.77.97). Hôtel de l'Horloge (05.63.39.91.61), tourist office.
  Small town on hilltop with circular medieval market hall, very well-restored, in arcaded square.   Church of Saint-Pierre, Romanesque Chapelle Sainte-Catherine, museum.

3.5km Bardigues (443.5/296.5)   Bar/restaurant by church (note that GR65 by-passes village).

4.5km Saint-Antoine (448/292)   No facilities except the gîte d'étape (05.62.28.64.27, 30pl., open all year, meals available, also CH), to R of road on leaving.
  Village takes its name from the religious order of the Antonins, who set up a hospital (the present château) for people suffering from ergotism, a disease also known as "St. Anthony's fire;" this was very prevalent in the Middle Ages, contracted by consuming cereal products (e.g. rye bread) contaminated by the ergot fungus and resulting in a gangrenous condition of hands and feet.   There was a similar such hospital further along the pilgrim road to Santiago in Spain shortly before Castrojeriz.
  You are now in the département of the Gers.

4km Flamarens (452/288)   *Village with castle (12th-15th c., a historic monument, still being restored   after many years but can be visited during July and August (10-12 and 14-19, except Tuesdays).*

[1km after Flamarens simple accomm. in caravan available at house of Xavier & Isabelle Ballenghien, La Patte d'Oie, 32340 Flamarens (*essential* to phone first: 05.62.28.61.13).   Note, however, that this is now off route as the course of the GR65 has been changed recently and now goes via Miradoux.]

1km before Miradoux, there are **two** *lieux -dits* (localities) named **Biran** (to R of GR): there is a CH and camping at the first, a small gîte d'étape (7pl., Mme Laville, 05.62.28.64.57) at the second.

4km Miradoux (456/284) Bar/restaurant, bakery, superette, bank (+CD), post office, pharmacy. On the Route de Valence, entering village, there is a Point d'Accueil and Info-Pèlerin at house on RH side with small pilgrim-only accommodation (8pl., no charge as such but leave donation: Thérèse Fardo, 05.62.28.66.57). Bar/Restaurant L'Etape also has a few rooms.
A village on historic route with Gothic church, Fontaine de Condé.

5km Castet-Arrouy (461/279) Gîte d'étape (18 pl., kitchen,), covered picnic area with pilgrim information opposite church and drinking water in cemetery opposite.
Church of Sainte-Blandine, begun in Gothic times with later additions has statues and newly restored 19th c. paintings (free guided tours daily May-Sept, 10-12, 15-19).

[The former route, now a *variante*, continued from here to Lectoure via **St. Avit-Frandat** (8.5km, 191m, bar with food and Château de Lacassagne, historic monument which includes a unique replica of the Great Council Chamber of the Knights of Jerusalem in Malta (visits possible).]

Gîte d'étape, 5pl., and CH (open all year) on GR itself, 4km after Castet-Arrouy and 6km before Lectoure at the Ferme Barrachin (Mme Esparbès, 05.62.68.68.84).

There is another gîte d'étape on GR 1km before Lectoure at the the *lieu-dit Tarisson*), 50m down track after crossing the N21 (ask next door for key, info. welcome).

10km Lectoure 186m (471/269) Pop. 4,000. All facilities. Gîte d'étape at 18 rue S. Gervais (22pl., open all year); key at tourist office (05.62.68.76.98) or Hôtel Le Bâtard (05.62.68.82.44) after hours. Pilgrim-only accommodation (8pl, eve. meal & bkft possible, donations) at presbytery in Hôtel des Trois Boules, 30 rue Nationale (05.62.68.83.83, Abbé Pierre Bourousse or Marc Boulade) but info. welcome as reports vary as to continued availability. The convent of the Soeurs de la Providence also has gîte-type accommodation (with kitchen). Hôtel Le Relais Saint-Jacques (05.62.68.83.79), also three CH: Mme Souviron (05.62.68.81.56), Mme Vetter (05.62.68.71.24) and Mme Luydlin (05.62.68.82.63).
One of the oldest towns in the Gers. Cathedral of SS Gervais & Protais, 17th-18th c. Hôtel de Ville, ramparts, many interesting old houses. (Lectoure is also a spa town.) Ask in tourist office for walking tour leaflet.

Pilgrims who decide they would rather cross the Pyrenees by the Somport pass and take the *Camino aragonés* to Puente la Reina can either leave the GR65 at Larreule (see below) or at Lectoure and then take the GR de Pays ("Coeur de Gascogne") south (approx. 35km) to join the GR653 at Saint-Cricq, to the east of Auch (hotels and campsites there and at Montestruc & Fleurance en route).

CH (and camping) Le Nauton-Saint-Jacques is 100m off GR, signposted to R 100m after a crossroads 1.5km before Marsolan (Mme Vincent, 05.62.68.99.81).

4.5km Marsolan 171m (480/260) *Remains of Hôpital Saint-Jacques at entrance to village.* Shady square behind church good place to rest. Covered rest area, phone box. CH and pilgrim gîte, open all year ex. July/Aug.,Mme Musset (05.62.68.79.40).

> *Note:.* After Marsolan there is a much shorter route direct to **Condom** (missing out La Romieu), waymarked in green. It continues straight on at the Chapelle d'Abrin (i.e. instead of turning R) along the valley of the river Auvignon and rejoins the GR65 500m after Castelnau.

5km Chapelle d'Abrin (485/255) *Former commandery of the Knights Hospitalers of St. John of Jerusalem (now a private house), pilgrim halt at meeting of two routes (the other came from Rocamadour and Moissac via Agen).*

Camping à la ferme de Gratzuzous (Mme Tichané, 05.62.28.44.54) 3km further on to R of GR off route also rents caravans per night.

5km La Romieu (490/250) Shop, café, shop, PTT, gîte d'étape (05.62.28.15.72 & 05.62.28.80.08, 19 pl., open all year, key from Mairie), tourist office (May-September). Restaurant-Camping Florence (outside town) has rooms in small bungalows. Both restaurants in centre, Le Relais des Arcades (05.62.28.10.29) and Le Cardinal (05.62.28.80.08) have rooms.
The village takes its name from the romieux (i.e. pilgrims) who passed through it on their way to Santiago. Like Condom and Lectoure, Le Romieu also has an enormous church for its size, an indication of its former importance: the 14th c. Collégiale (built by Clement V, one of the Avignon Popes) with 2 large towers, double cloister and frescoed chapel is well worth a visit.

6.5km Chapelle Sainte-Germaine de Soldanum 168m (496.5/243.5) *12th-13th c. chapel, all that remains of former monastery (destroyed in the 9th century by the Normans) dedicated to a local saint. Now being restored ,the church is normally open when the cemetery is.*
1km before Condom (signposted from GR65) is the Centre équestre L'Etrier Condomois with CH (M. Defrancès, 05.62.28.23.80, pilgrim rate).

9.5km Condom 81m (506/234) Pop. 8,000. All facilities, tourist office, gîte d'étape in Centre Salvandry, 20 Rue Jean Jaures (6 pl., open all year), municipal campsite by river (April-October). Basic gîte reported at Earl du Laillon (05.62.28.19.71). Hôtel Relais de la Ténarèze (05.62.28.02.54), Hôtel des Trois Lys (05.62.28.33.33), Hôtel des Cordeliers (05.62.28.03.68).

Typical Gascon town situated on a spur between the river Gèle and the river Baïse, centre of the Armagnac industry. Well preserved centre with cathedral of Saint-Pierre, Musée de l'Armagnac, cloisters (now the mairie) On the other side of the river is the church of Saint-Jacques, which originally had a hospital attached to it (but note that the statue above the blocked-up doorway on the street side is not St. James but St. Joseph, a dedication made in recognition of the latter's help in alleviating the sufferings of plague victims in that quarter of the town, La Bouguerie.)

5km Le Carbon 179m (511/229) To visit **Larresingle**, a tiny fortified town 1km off route, completely walled (restaurant, Auberge de Larresingle, 7 rooms, 05.62.28.29.67), turn R along road at Le Carbon. This was the fortress of the Bishops of Condom in the Middle Ages and is well worth the 15 minute detour (in each direction) to visit. To return, however, you need not retrace your steps again but, via a minor road to the SW you can pick up the GR65 where it crosses the D278, just before the Pont d'Artigues, turning R to cross it.

3km Pont d'Artigues (514/226) *Originally a Roman bridge over the Osse, with five arches. In the Middle Ages there was a pilgrim hospital belonging, successively, to the Diocese of Santiago, the Knights of the Order of Santiago and then the order of Saint-Jacques-de-la-Foi-et-de-la-Paix but there is no trace of it left today. There was also a church of Notre-Dame by the pilgrim bridge but nothing remains of this today either.*

2.5km Eglise de Routges (516.5/223.5) *100m ahead of you, off road, is the oldest church in the region. Note the small door on the side of the church: this was the entrance used by the Cagots, an outcast population.*

6.5km Montréal du Gers 135m (523/217) Shops, café, restaurant, tourist office, PTT. Hôtel Saint-Jacques down hill at western end of town (05.62.29.43.07).

Small bastide town (population 1,200) with arcaded market place, 13th c. church, several interesting old houses, museum, ramparts.

Gallo-Roman villa at **Seviac** (2km, worth visiting) also has a gîte d'étape (05.62.29.48.57, 14pl., 1/3-30/11 though it may be full if a "dig" is in progress) and CH next to site (Mme Cahuzac, 05.62.29.44.12). 300m away pilgrims can also sleep in a fully equipped mobile home (phone ahead, M & Mme Labeyre, 05.62.29.45.77 or 06.14.44.60.64). New private gîte also reported.

9km Lamothe 167m (532/208) 13th c. guard tower. Gîte équestre on GR after 3km at Escoubet (05.62.09.93.03, open all year).

7km Eauze 142m (539/201) Population 4300. Shops, cafés, several restaurants, PTT. Gîte d'étape (pilgrims only) opposite tourist office (05.62.09.85.62 & 06.85.17.65.15, 14pl., 1/3 - 30/11); municipal campsite (July & August). Hôtel de l'Armagnac (05.62.09.88.11), Le Grand Hôtel (closed Mondays, 05.62.09.85.62) and Hôtel Henri IV (05.62.09.75.90).

Former Gallor-Roman capital (Elusa) and Roman colony. Benedictine priory founded in 10th century and attached to Order of Cluny. Church of Saint-Luperc (a local saint) built by the Benedictines, finished 1521, using rubble stone from Roman sites mixed with local brick. Contains two 17th c. confessionals and, in side chapel, statue of Saint-Roch pilgrim and stained glass windows of Saint-Jacques (apse) and Saint-Roch (south wall). Icons on long centre panel behind altar are modern (1977), by Nicholaï Greschny (Tarn artist). Numerous old houses, including Maison de Jeanne d'Albret, Museum (with treasury of 28,000 Roman coins), Andalusian-style bull-ring (Arènes Nimeño II).

7km Ferme de Peyret 160m (546/194) Turn R here for gite d'étape in old school in *Sauboires*, 800m further, turn R here (05.62.08.52.99, 10pl., all yr).

4km Manciet (550/190) Shops, gîte d'étape (05.62.08.58.11, 7pl., camping possible). Bar/restaurant des Sports Chez Monique has rooms and another gîte (10 pl., 05.62.08.56.40). Hôtel-restaurant La Bonne Auberge (05.62.08.50.04) is on *site of former commandery (with Hôpital Saint-Jacques and chapel) set up by the Spanish Ordre Hospitalier de Santiago (i.e. Knights of Santiago).*

Rural bullring for courses landaises (cattle races). Church of Notre-Dame de la Pitié has "viewing kiosk" and prayer desk accessible from the street when church is closed and modern bas-relief of Saint-Jacques above door and statue of Saint-Roch inside.

3km Eglise-hôpital Sainte-Christie (553/187) *This is the church of Saint-Jean-Baptiste de la Commanderie de Sainte-Christie de l'Armagnac, formerly belonging to the Order of the Knights of Malta (a milestone with a Maltese Cross is to be found 50m after the church, on the waymarked variant returning you to the D522). The 300m detour from GR worth the effort for its silence and simplicity ; key to the church i s normally available for an inside visit.*

To continue you do not need to retrace your steps but can turn R 50m past the church (waymarked with yellow and red arrows), turn L and then R up hill up side of field for 100m. Turn L (before top of hill) onto FP through trees, leading to field. Turn L and at corner of field go down steps (L) leading to the D522 where you turn L along it to continue.

Gîte at **Monneton**, 250m off GR (signed with snail waymarks), 15 pl., run by former pilgims Geneviève & Gaston, 10 euros, kitchen or meals avail. (05.62.08.82.61, good reports).

6km Nogaro 98m (559/181) Population 2,000. All facilities, 3 hotels, municipal gîte d'étape (on GR leaving town, 05.62.69.06.15, 17pl., some 2 bed rooms, open all year), campsite (next to gîte, June-September). CH (M. Malibos, 05.62.09.13.17), Hôtel Le Commerce (05.62.09.00.95) and Hôtel Les Arènes (05.62.09.03.33), tourist office.
Small town taking its name from "Nogarium" (a "place planted with walnuts") and established in the 11th century. Romanesque church with former Hôpital Saint-Jacques nearby. Bullring.
Note: a) the GR65 does not enter the town and b) there are no shops or cafés till you reach either Barcelonne-du-Gers, 23km away, or Aire-sur-l'Adour, 27km away, so buy supplies before you leave Nogaro.

10km Lanne-Soubiran (565/175) CH Mme Martet (05.62.69.04.19).

[If you want to go to **Barcelonne-du-Gers**, 2km off route on D935, 23km after Nogaro and 6km before Aire sur l'Adour, KSO after **Lacassagne** (a farm) then turn R 1km later onto D107. Hôtel-restaurant chez Alain (05.62.09.44.39), another bar/restaurant, supermarket. To return to the GR go back along the D107 and continue to the Pont sur l'Adour.
CH off route at "Le Glindon" (Mme Carlin, 05.62.08.97.61, reported excellent) will also collect (and return) you from/to phone box in Barcelonne du Gers.]

17m Pont sur l'Adour (586/154) Camping municipal Rives de l'Adour by bridge (05.62.09.47.60, 15/6-15/9; also rents caravans per night).
Note: the GR65 does not enter Aire-sur-l'Adour but takes a high-level detour, joining up with the route through the town on the N134 on the outskirts 2km beyond the centre. If you want to go into the town KSO past the first turn on the L (waymarked), on the road, into the town centre. *To go directly to the gîte d'étape (in the Centre de Loisirs, Quartier de la Plaine):* turn R down the *Chemin de la Plaine* 150m after the pavement begins at entry to town.

2km Aire-sur-l'Adour 81m (588/152) Pop. 6,200, all facilities. Gîte d'étape in Centre de Loisirs (05.58.71.61.63, 60pl., open all year; essential to reserve as often full with groups). Campsite by river behind tourist office (Les Ombrages de l'Adour, 05.58.71.64.70 & 05.58.71.75.10, May-September, also rents caravans per night). 5 hotels, including Hôtel de la Paix (05.58.71.60.70) which has a special (cheap) pilgrim price (10 euros, including breakfast), CH (Mme Fage, 05.58.71.63.03). CH also at Quartier de Guillon (Mme Porte, 5km off route, who will collect you from town centre if you phone a few days ahead, 05.58.71.91.73, reported good, meals). CRS: A. Aladu, 22 rue Pascal Duprat.

Ancient town in two parts: the lower section by the river with the cathedral of Saint- Jean Baptiste (12th century but altered several times), mairie, 19th c. Halle aux Grains and former religious courts of justice and the "Mas d'Aire" or higher town with the brick built Eglise de Sainte-Quitterie built on site of Benedictine monastery (ask for guided tour, reported good)..
Petrol station on leaving town has bar/shop.

Off route, at **Geaune**, pilgrims can sleep in Centre Parroissial (2 beds) 50m from church (05.58.44.51.82; info welcome).

New gîte reported 8km south of Aire-sur-l'Adour: Mme Lepinay, Gîte Talazac, (05.62.09.42.49; they will collect you from centre of Aire-sur-l'Adour if necessary).

13.5km Latrille (601.5/138.5) Drinking water in churchyard, phone box.

6km Miramont-Sensacq (607.5/132.5) Gîte d'étape (05.58.79.91.23 & 05.58.79.93.84, 8pl., open all year), bakery, shop. Hôtel Beaumont (with bar-restaurant, 05.58.79.90.65, closed Mondays but unreliable opening hours also reported).

4.5km Eglise de Sensacq 149m (612/128) New private gîte (dormitory and rooms) at Maison Marsan (05.58.79.94.93). *11th.c. church formerly dedicated to Saint James. Contains total immersion font (for infants) in NW corner. Vestibule-style enclosed porch with some benches (useful for rest).*

2.5km Pimbo 190m (614.5/125.5) Fountain (drinking water). Pilgrims can sleep in Foyer Rural or Mairie (phone first: 05.58.44.49.18) but reports vary. CH M. Lendresse (05.58.44.49.23 and 05.58.44.46.92). *Acceuil pèlerin* in church most afternoons (summer only?) that sells drinks, gives tour of church and stamps pilgrim passports.
One of the oldest bastide villages in the Landes, founded c. 1268, with collegiate church of Saint-Barthélemy on site of monastery founded by Charlemagne. Water available at farm 1km after Pimbo.

6.5km Arzacq-Arraziguet 231m(621/119) Shops, cafés, restaurant, bank (+CD), 2 hotels. Gîte d'étape and campsite in Centre d'Accueil (05.59.04.41.41, 70pl., meals possible, open all year). Hôtel-restaurant La Vieille Auberge (05.59.04.51.31). You have now left Les Landes and have entered the *département* of the Pyrénées-Atlantiques.
Bastide town with 2 main squares, side by side, founded by "les Anglais" in 13th-14th c., Arzacq was in France at that time, not in the Béarn (a separate country). (Note names of rivers in the area: Luy-de-Béarn and Luy-de-France). Arzacq used to mark the boundary between France and the (then independant)

Béarn country. Parish church of Saint-Pierre has stained glass window of St. James.

4km Louvigny (625/115) *Modern church of Saint-Martin replaces original church belonging to château formerly existing above the village in hamlet of Lou Castet: the remains of castle and church were only demolished during the twentieth century. One stained glass window in new church contains coquille and pilgrim staff and gourd.*

8km Larreule (633/107) *Site of a Benedictine monastery founded about 995 and which was an an important pilgrim stage in the Middle Ages, with church of Saint-Pierre, partly Romanesque. (The name Larreule means "La Règle" (i.e. monastic rule) in Gascon, a name also found elsewhere, near Maubouget on the Arles route and in La Réole on the Vézelay route.)*
Garden adjoining church is a nice place for a rest.

Pilgrims who decide they would rather cross the Pyrenees by the Somport pass and take the *Camino aragonés* to Puente la Reina can leave the GR65 here and continue on minor roads to join the GR653 (the Arles route) at Lescar.

3km Uzan (636/104) Spartan gîte accommodation available in Foyer Rural (key in Mairie or from 05.59.81.69.2).
Church of Sainte-Quitterie, Fontaine Sainte-Quitterie on other side of road (a saint very revered in the area).

4km Pomps (640/100) Bar/restaurant, shop. Spartan gîte accommodation, (showers, 20 vaulting mats, no cooking) available in sports hall (05.59.81.65.12, open all year).
Church of Saint-Jacques (with statue of the saint), château with octagonal tower.
4.5km Castillon 198m (644.5/95.5) *Hospital for pilgrims and travellers in 11th c. church of Saint-Pierre.*

2.5km Chapelle de Caubin (647/93) *Restored Romanesque chapel on the site of the remains of a former Commandery of the Knights of Saint John. Garden opposite (picnic tables) contains a sculpture recalling the passage of pilgrims en route to Santiago.*

2km Arthez-de-Béarn 211m (649/91) Shops, bank (+CD), cafés, restaurant, no hotel but two rooms reported over *boulangerie*. Basic municipal gîte d'étape (05.59.67.70.52, 19 pl., open all year) and another one in preparation. CRS.
A very long town along a ridge (nearly 2km from one end to the other), originally

developed around the Augustinian commandery whose monastery was destroyed in the Wars of Religion. Several interesting old houses, ramparts. Note transition towards Basque-style architecture.

7km Eglise d'Argagnon (656/84) Municipal gîte d'étape off route in village, 4pl, open all year (05.59.67.60.59).

2km Maslacq (658/82) Shop, hotel/restaurant, small gîte d'étape in town centre (4pl., open all year, 05.59.67.60.79, ask at Mairie) though reports vary; facilities are all in separate places and keys (and good French) may be needed to get them all unlocked; info., welcome. Hôtel Maugouber (05.59.38.78.00) is now a "Logis de France" and is expensive but has reasonably priced restaurant.

8km La Sauvelade (666/74) Municipal gîte d'étape next to abbey (05.59.67.60.59 & 05.59.67.61.32, 19pl., open all year), no shops. CH (Mme Grosclaude, 05.59.67.60.57).
   The church is all that remains of the monastery, originally Benedictine, founded by Gaston IV of Béarn in 1128, and later Cistercian. It was sacked by the Huguenots in 1569, restored after 1630 and then sold off at the time of the French Revolution. The church was built between 1215 and 1250, originally dedicated to Saint Mary but later changed to Saint James the Great, in recognition of all the pilgrims who rested in the abbey. Statue of Saint James inside.

12km Navarrenx 125m (678/62) Pop. 1,500. All facilities. Municipal gîte d'étape in former Arsenal building near Hôtel de Ville (05.59.66.10.22, 15pl., April to 1/11); key from Mme Lasarrocques (who also does good meals) at Bar du Centre (05.59.66.50.78) nearby. New private gîte on outskirts of town in Cami Dou Mouli (12 pl. in dormitory + CH, 05.59.66.07.25 and 06.08.93.56.41). Campsite by river (April-September). Hôtel du Commerce (05.59.66.50.16), Bar des Sports has rooms (05.59.66.50.63, closed August, also CH).
   Note: accomodation is no longer available at the presbytery as Abbé Ihidoy has now moved away from Navarrenx but between Easter and November pilgrims who wish can attend prayers and a tour of the church there at 6pm followed by a verre d'amitié in the presbytery at 18.30 offered by the parish.
   First town in France to be fortified with Italian-style ramparts (16th c.): ask at tourist office for town plan with walking tour. Church of Saint-Germain, finished 1562 but a Protestant temple till 1620 when it was reconverted to a Catholic church (note pilgrim boss in ceiling near side chapel to RH side, with head with leather hat and cockle shell). In former times Navarrenx also had a significant Cagot (outcast) population, several of whom became prominent public figures.

CH and gîte équestre 1km before Aroue at the **Ferme Bohoteguya** (where the GR65 joins the D11) (8pl, 40FF, bkft 10FF, kitchen), CH (meals avail., including vegetarian, if booked ahead: 05.59.65.85.69) and campsite. Farm produce for sale. Reports vary. (Is this still open?)

19km Aroue (697/43) Small municipal gîte d'étape (05.59.65.95.54, 6pl., open all year), near bar/tabac in petrol station. Mme Lagarde at end of village does eve. meal (reported very copious) on request (05.59.65.60.16).
Romanesque church of Saint-Etienne has 12th c. bas reliefs with Santiago Matamoros in lintel above sacristy doors.

If you want to take the alternative route via **Saint-Palais** you can either continue from Aroue on the D11 (10km) or turn off the GR65 9km later when you reach the **Ferme de Benta**: KSO at farm on minor road to *Quinquilemia*, continuing through **Uruxondoa** and **Béhasque-Lapiste**, turning L onto the D11 to Saint-Palais at **Quintalena** (7km).

Saint-Palais (Donapaleu) Pop.2,000, all facilities, campsite (June-Sept.). Hôtel du Midi (05.59.65.70.64), Hôtel de la Paix (05.59.65.73.15), Hôtel de la Gare (05.59.65.73.25), L'Auberge du Foirail (05.59.65.73.22) and Hôtel du Trinquet (05.59.65.73.13). CRS: S.O. Cyclon, Avenue de la Ville, near *frontón* (pelota court).
Pilgrims can stay in Maison franciscaine "Zabalik," 1 Avenue de Gibraltar, on way out of town leading back to GR65 (05.59.65.71.37, 14 pl., open all year, prior reservation strongly advised; evening meal and breakfast provided (arrive by 6,45pm). Very welcoming. No charge as such but you should leave a donation. Morning mass (in Basque) in chapel.
Typical Franco-Basque town with pilgrim museum, Musée de la Basse Navarre et des Chemins de Saint-Jacques de Compostelle, next to Mairie (visit recommended), started by Dr. Urrutibéhéty who used to be the local doctor but who is now better known as an expert on the pilgrim route .
You can pick up the GR65 again at *Hiriburia* by taking the D302 south and continuing on the road.
CH at **Aicivits**, close to St. Palais on pilgrim route from Sauveterre-de-Béarn (M. Escondeur, 05.59.65.65.54).

12km Larribar-Sorhapuru 89m (709/31) Café. *Shrine to R of path with small statue of Saint-Jacques behind glass in a stèle and also water-colour of church under glass.*

2km Hiriburia 151m (711/29) *A few metres to the R, where the routes from Paris, Vézelay and Le Puy are thought to have met, the Société des Amis de Saint-Jacques have erected a small monument. If you look at its "feet" and at those marked "Ostabat" you will also see where you are going next: up the clear track uphill in front of you, the "Chemin de procession" leading up to the Chapelle*

de Soyarza, *300m, a modern building replacing a much older oratory dedicated to Notre-Dame. Adjoining the chapel is a covered rest area with pilgrim book (water available). Superb views all round from the top on a clear day.*
Note: you can also go to *Saint-Palais* from Hiribiria, 3km.

3km Harambeltz (714/26) *Site of former Benedictine priory-hospital of Saint Nicholas. The 1000 year old chapel remains and has a clocher trinitaire (three-pronged belfry), the only one on the Le Puy route, and an 18th c. altarpiece and statue of Saint James but it belongs to the families in the village and is not a parish church. It is difficult to visit though the door (but not the grille) is sometimes open, enabling you to see inside. Note interesting old houses in the village.*

5km Ostabat-Asme (Izura) 124m (719/21) 2 bars, shop, restaurant, CH, gîte d'étape in lower part of town (05.59.37.83.17, 16pl., April-November, (key with M. Etchepareborde next door). Restaurant Arbeletch has rooms (05.59.37.85.03). CH and gîte 1km outside village on GR at Ferme Gaineko-Extea (Mme Eyharts, 20pl., 05.59.37.81.10 and 06.72.73.78.56, reported good, open all year).

Ostabat is a small village today but in the past it was an important gathering point for pilgrims coming from or along different routes. In the Middle Ages its hospitals and inns could accommodate up to 5000 pilgrims but today only the Maison Ospetalia remains and is now the gîte d'étape.

There are no big pilgrim monuments in the French Basque country but there were formerly many small hospitals and chapels (in Harambeltz and Itziat, for example).

4km Larceveau (Larzabale) 160m (723/17) Hotel-restaurant Espellet (05.59.37.81.91) and Hôtel-restaurant Trinquet (05.59.37.81.59), pharmacy, shop.

13km Saint-Jean-le-Vieux (Donazaharre) 212m (736/4) Shops, cafés, restaurants, Hôtel Mendy (05.59.37.11.81) with campsite, CH (M. Esponde, 05.59.37.08.21).

Pilgrims originally went straight from Saint-Jean-le-Vieux to Saint-Michel (the route described in Aymery Picard's twelfth-century guidebook). The deviation via Saint-Jean-de-Pied-de-Port developed from the 13th century onwards. Church of Saint- Pierre affiliated to the Augustinian Canons in Roncesvalles until 14th century.

Campsite (March-September) to RH side of GR at Quartier de la Madeleine, 2km before Saint- ean-Pied-de-Port.

4km Saint-Jean-de-Pied-de-Port (Donibane Garazi) 180m (740/0)
Population 1,400. All facilities. Pilgrim information office (Acceuil Pèlerin de

l'Association des Amis de Saint-Jacques des Pyrénées Atlantiques) is run by volunteers, mainly former pilgrims, at 39 Rue de la Citadelle, open March-November, early morning to evening, and provides information on the route in Spain, helps with accommodation, provides pilgrim passports where appropriate and stamps them; it is suggested you call there as soon as you arrive in Saint-Jean-Pied-de-Port. tourist office, SNCF (to Bayonne).

Gîtes d'étape: a) Mme Etchegoin, 9 Rue d'Huart (05.59.37.12.08, 12 pl.), b) (pilgrims only) Rue de la Citadelle (16 pl., March-November, access via Accueil Pèlerin), c) 'L'Esprit du Chemin," 18-20 pl., open 1/4-30/9, run by two former pilgrims from Holland, Huberta Wiertsema and Arno Cuppen, no kitchen but serves reasonably priced meals, 40 Rue de la Citadelle (05,59.37.15.64), d) 21 Rue d'Espagne, Mme Hitte (05.59.37.20.71). Campsite by river (1/4-15/10). Seven hotels (mainly expensive) including Camou (05.59.37.02.78), Remparts (05.59.37.13.79), Itzalpea (05.59.37.03.66) & Ramuntcho (05.59.37.03.91). Several CH including Mme Camino (sic, 15 Rue de la Citadelle, 05.59.37.05.83), Mme Cléry (28 Rue de la Citadelle, 05.59.37.12.03), M. Etchegoin (11 Route de l'Uhart, 05.59.37.07.08), Mme Garicoitz (05.59.37.06.46) and M. Chateauneuf (05.59.37.32.08).

This is "Saint John-at-the-Foot-of-the-Pass," a small border town on the river Nive, capital of the Basque province of Basse Navarre with an ancient cobbled "haute ville." Several places of interest: Citadelle, overlooking the town, with its system of ramparts: access either from the top end of the Rue de la Citadelle or by staircase ("escalier de la poterne") leading up from the footpath along the river by the side of the church - worth the climb on a clear day. Prison des Evêques, Musée de la Pelote, 14th c. Eglise Notre-Dame-du-bout-du-pont ("Our Lady at the end of the bridge," part of the former priory-hospital). Pont Romain, the different "portes" (Saint-Jacques, d'Espagne, for example). Note architecture of Basque-style houses with often ornate wooden overhangs at roof level, balconies. If you have time to spare the tourist office has a booklet of waymarked walks in the area.

Traditionally pilgrims entered the town by the Porte Saint-Jacques at the top of the Rue de la Citadelle and those who have followed the GR65 will have done the same. After that there were two routes to Roncevaux/Roncesvalles. The older one, following the course of the river *Nive*, is now the modern road (D933 in France, N135 in Spain). This route is no shorter but is not so steep. It is on the main road for most of the first 15km but if the weather is very bad or visibility poor you should take this. [Gîtes d'étape 4km out of Saint-Jean-Pied-de-Port on this route, at Moulin de Fargas (05.59.37.12.54, 22pl.) and at Mendi Beherria, on the Route de Arnéguy (Mme Cotabarren, 05.59.37.36.26). Arnéguy (Arnegi) has shop, cafés and restaurant, as does Valcarlos (which also has a *pensión* and 2 hotels).

The other, high-level *Route Napoléon* was the one he took to cross into Spain, following existing tracks already used by shepherds and pilgrims for several centuries. This leads over the Pyrenees via the *Col de Bentarte* and the *Port de Cize*, continuing along the path of the old Roman road from Bordeaux to Astorga, and is normally accessible without any trouble (i.e. too much snow) from May to October. It is 26km long and is a spectacular route on a clear day but do not attempt it if it is already very windy down below in Saint-Jean-Pied-de-Port; higher up you can experience force nine gales and appalling weather, even in the height of summer. [Note, however, that there is a gîte d'étape (plus CH) 5km out of St. Jean, at Honto (Huntto); 05.59.37.11.17, 25pl.] The Route Napoléon was also the one favoured by pilgrims in centuries gone by because, although it was much more strenuous, it was also exposed for most of the way, and they were thus less likely to be ambushed by bandits than on the densely wooded route through Valcarlos. If you are a fairly fit walker allow at least seven hours actual walking (excluding stops); if not, allow much longer, especially if it is windy (when it will almost always be against you).

However, start early in the day whichever route you take (e.g. 6.30 in summer or as soon as it is light), not only to avoid the heat but also being high up later in the day when the light is fading and you are tired. If you choose the Route Napoléon take *enough food and water* with you, including (both routes) the following morning's breakfast.

If you are continuing to end/break your journey in Pamplona you may like to know that there is a *refugio* in **Roncesvalles** (26km, 2 bar-restaurants and other hotel accommodation, CD in lobby of monastery-run Posada), *hostal* accommodation in **Burgete** (3km after Roncesvalles), and *refugios* in **Zubiri** (22km + shop, hostal, restaurant), **Larrasoana** (6km, restaurant) and **Trinidad de Arre** (12km, shops etc., in outer suburbs of Pamplona, 4km from centre).

* * * * * * *

NOTES